These six essays will be of great interest to all students of liturgy, dealing as they do with various aspects of the Roman liturgy during a formative period. Dr Willis deals with such varied subjects as the solemn prayers of Good Friday, the Ember Days, *Mediana* week, the offertory prayers and the Canon of the Mass, the *Cursus* and the connection of prayers in the Canon. These subjects are examined with the scholarly care and attention to detail we have already met in Dr Willis's reconstruction of *St Augustine's Lectionary*.

ESSAYS IN EARLY ROMAN LITURGY

ALCUIN CLUB COLLECTIONS
No. XLVI

Essays in Early Roman Liturgy

G. G. WILLIS

Published for the Alcuin Club

BX 1970 W5 1964 glas
Willis, Geoffrey Grimshaw.
Essays in early Roman liturgy.

Computer ID: 54567

LONDON
S · P · C · K
1964

First published in 1964
by S.P.C.K.
Holy Trinity Church
Marylebone Road
London N.W.1

Printed in Great Britain by
Billing & Sons Ltd., Guildford and London

© G. G. Willis, 1964

Contents

Preface

The essays here collected are on subjects concerning the Roman rite in the early Middle Ages which, so far as I know, have not attracted the attention of English writers to any notable extent during the present century, but which have seemed worthy of investigation.

Essays III and V were first read as papers to the first and second summer meetings of the Ecclesiastical History Society at Cambridge in 1962 and 1963. They are related to the other four essays, and it was therefore thought convenient to print them here. They are, however, to appear in *Studies in Ecclesiastical History* I and II, and I am grateful to the President of the Ecclesiastical History Society for the year 1963–4, the Reverend Professor C. W. Dugmore, and to the publishers, Messrs. Thomas Nelson and Sons, Ltd, for kindly giving permission to reprint them. I am also indebted to the Right Reverend the Lord Abbot of Mont-César for leave to reproduce the critical text of the *Deprecatio Gelasii* prepared by his predecessor, the late Dom Bernard Capelle (to whom students of Roman liturgy owe so much), and which was originally printed in the *Revue Bénédictine* and reproduced in Dom Capelle's collected papers, *Travaux liturgiques*, published by the Centre Liturgique, Mont-César, Louvain.

My thanks are also due to Professor G. D. Kilpatrick and Dr F. J. E. Raby, who both read the typescript and suggested notable improvements in it, delivering me also from sundry errors and omissions; and to the Alcuin Club for accepting the book as Collection No. XLVI.

Wing Vicarage, Bucks. GEOFFREY G. WILLIS
13 *June* 1964.

Abbreviations

C.C.	Corpus Christianorum, Turnhoult.
C.S.E.L.	Corpus Scriptorum Ecclesiasticorum Latinorum, Vienna.
D.A.C.L.	Dictionnaire d'archéologie chrétienne et de liturgie, Paris.
E.L.	Ephemerides Liturgicae, Rome.
H.B.S.	Henry Bradshaw Society, London.
J.T.S.	*Journal of Theological Studies*, Oxford.
L.E.W.	F. E. Brightman, *Liturgies Eastern and Western*, Oxford.
Q.L.P.	*Les Questions liturgiques et paroissiales*, Louvain.
P.G.	Patrologiae Series Graeca, ed. J. P. Migne, Paris.
P.L.	Patrologiae Series Latina, ed. J. P. Migne, Paris.
R.B.	*Revue Bénédictine*, Maredsous.
R.H.E.	*Revue d'histoire ecclésiastique*, Louvain.

I

The Solemn Prayers of Good Friday

1. *The Prayer of the Faithful*

When St Justin Martyr is describing the baptismal mass of the middle of the second century, he says that the neophyte is led from the font to the brethren, who are assembled for prayer, which they are about to offer on behalf of themselves, of the neophyte, and of all men everywhere. These "common prayers", κοιναὶ εὐχαί, are followed by the kiss of peace and by the anaphora.[1] The "common prayers" are mentioned also by St Justin in a description of the ordinary Sunday mass, where they occur in the same place, after the Sermon and before the Anaphora.[2] Half a century later, Hippolytus, in the *Apostolic Tradition*, written about 215, mentions that the neophytes pray with all the people immediately after their baptism, and that they are not permitted to do this before they are baptized.[3]

It is clear from these two accounts that the Intercession belongs to the Mass of the Faithful, and not to that of the Catechumens, and that it is the first item in the Mass of the Faithful, and comes before the great Eucharistic Prayer or Anaphora. St Justin is the earliest witness to the intercession in this position anywhere in Christendom. Because it belongs to the Mass of the Faithful, and is not uttered in the presence of the catechumens, it acquired the title of the Prayer of the Faithful (*Oratio fidelium*), which seems to be echoed in the words of Hippolytus, *orantes cum fidelibus*.

These two pieces of evidence of the intercession of the mass are from Rome. But we have fairly early evidence of the same practice from Egypt and Africa. Origen, at the beginning of the third century, describes them as *oratio communis*.[4] A phrase in Tertullian about

[1] Justin, *Apol.*, i, 65, in *Iustini opera*, ed. I. C. T. Otto, Ienae, 1876, pp. 176, 178.

[2] Ibid., p. 186.

[3] *Didascaliae apostolorum fragmenta ueronensia latina*, LXXIII–LXXIV, ed. E. Hauler, Leipzig, 1900, pp. 111–12: et postea [i.e. after baptism and confirmation] iam simul cum omni populo orent, non primum orantes cum fidelibus nisi omnia haec fuerint consecuti. et cum orauerint de ore pacem offerant. et tunc iam offeratur oblatio a diaconibus episcopo.

[4] Orig., *In Matt.*, xxvi, 36; ed. Erich Klostermann, *Origines Werke*, elfter Band, *Origenes Matthäuserklärung*, II, *Die lateinische Übersetzung der Commentariorum Series*, Leipzig, 1933, p. 205.

prayer for prisoners may be a reference to one of the subjects of such a general intercession.[1] His disciple, St Cyprian, refers to prayers for the *lapsi* and the *stantes*, which may well have formed two petitions of such prayers of the faithful.[2] Baumstark traces the origin of the particular form of this intercession which is seen in the Roman Solemn Prayers of Good Friday to the time of St Cyprian.[3]

From Egypt we have the text of some prayers by the faithful for various orders in the Church, for the afflicted, and for kings, from the Sacramentary of Serapion, who was Bishop of Thmuis in the Delta about 350.[4] The treatise of St Ambrose *De sacramentis* gives evidence from Milan in the last quarter of the fourth century, to the effect that before the consecration prayers of intercession were offered for the people, for kings, and for other needs.[5]

General intercessions form part of all Eastern rites.[6] Usually they occur in the same position as the Roman *Orationes Sollemnes* and the intercessions referred to by Justin Martyr, that is at the beginning of the Mass of the Faithful, or Anaphora. There is an intercession at this place in the Syrian Liturgy of the eighth book of the Apostolic Constitutions, after the penitents and catechumens have been dismissed;[7] in the Egyptian Liturgy of St Mark, after the Gospel, at the beginning of the Anaphora;[8] in the Liturgy of the Coptic Jacobites, at the beginning of the Anaphora;[9] in the Persian Liturgy of the Nestorians, at the beginning of the Anaphora.[10]

Eastern liturgies have a habit, however, of repeating the Intercessions twice or even three times: thus the Liturgy of the eighth book of the Apostolic Constitutions, of the Coptic Jacobites, and of the Abyssinian Jacobites have each three intercessions; and those of St James, St Mark, and the Nestorians, have two. When the intercession does not come in the Roman position at the beginning of the Mass of the Faithful, or

[1] Tert., *De Oratione*, 29; P.L. I, 1303; C.S.E.L. XX, 199; C.C. I, 274: Itaque nihil nouit (oratio) nisi . . . claustra carceris aperire . . .

[2] Cypr., *Ep.*, XXXI, 6; P.L. IV, 321; C.S.E.L. III, 562.

[3] A. Baumstark, *Comparative Liturgy*, revised by Bernard Botte, E.T. by F. L. Cross, London, 1958, pp. 77–8; "Liturgischer Nachhall der Verfolgungszeit" in Albert Michael Koeniger, *Beiträge zur Geschichte des christlichen Altertums und der byzantinischen Literatur, Festgabe Albert Ehrhard*, Bonn-Leipzig, 1922, pp. 53–72.

[4] Nos. XXII–XXV, ed. G. Wobbermin, in *Texte und Untersuchungen*, XVII, Heft 3*b*, pp. 16–18, Leipzig, 1898.

[5] Ambr., *De sacramentis*, IV, iv, 14; P.L. XVI, 440; C.S.E.L. LXXXIII, 52.

[6] The following references are to F. E. Brightman, *Liturgies Eastern and Western, I, Eastern Liturgies*, Oxford, 1896.

[7] Pp. 9–12. [8] 119–120. [9] 159–61. [10] 262–5.

Anaphora, it tends to come at the very beginning of the Mass of the Catechumens, in the position in which Gelasius inserted his Litany or *Deprecatio*; or else in the midst of the Anaphora, in a position comparable to the intercessions of the latest form of the Roman rite, *Te igitur* and the two *Mementos*. Thus the Liturgy of the eighth book of the Apostolic Constitutions has an intercession at the beginning of the Anaphora, after the dismissal of the catechumens,[1] another in the Anaphora before the Inclination, Elevation, and Communion,[2] and a third at the Inclination.[3] St James has one after the kiss of peace, at the Inclination,[4] and another between the Invocation and the Lord's Prayer.[5] In Egypt the Liturgy of St Mark has one after the Gospel,[6] and one after the Thanksgiving, near the beginning of the Anaphora;[7] the Coptic Jacobites have one after the Gospel,[8] one at the beginning of the Anaphora,[9] and one within the Anaphora after the Preface;[10] and the Abyssinian Jacobites have a deacon's litany before the mass of the catechumens,[11] one after the Preface,[12] and one after the Inclination.[13] The Nestorians have one after the dismissal of the catechumens,[14] and one at the Diptychs, before the Anaphora.[15] In the Byzantine rite of St Basil there is only one intercession, which occurs after the Invocation, and this is a long prayer, not a deacon's litany interrupted by the people's response. The intercession of the Armenian Liturgy occurs near the beginning of the mass of the catechumens.

In almost all cases the intercessions are in the form of litanies precented by the deacon, to which the people respond *Kyrie eleison*, and the petitions are often, though not always, very short, simply asking prayers for various classes of people. All eastern intercessions are remarkable for the great number of classes of people for whom they pray. If the Liturgy of St James may be taken as an example, the first intercession after the kiss of peace[16] prays for peace from above and salvation; for the peace of the world; for the whole Church; for our orthodox kings, their palace, and army; for our city; for almsgivers and succourers of the needy and strangers; for all old and weak people; for those possessed by evil spirits; for virgins, ascetics, and matrons; for sailors, travellers, prisoners, exiles, and slaves; for the present congregation; for all Christians in tribulation; for the erring, the sick, prisoners, and the faithful departed; for fine weather and showers and dew; good fruit and the "crown of the year", or harvest. Then the

[1] Brightman, *L.E.W.*, 9–12. [2] 21–2. [3] 23. [4] 44–6. [5] 54–6. [6] 119–20. [7] 126–30. [8] 157. [9] 159–61. [10] 165–74. [11] 206–8. [12] 229–30. [13] 236. [14] 262–5. [15] 236. [16] 44–6.

intercession between the Invocation and the Lord's Prayer prays again for the same kind of thing;[1] for the whole Church; the Bishops; the celebrant and the deacons; all orthodox cities; kings, queens, the palace, and the army; sailors, travellers, prisoners, slaves, exiles, those in the mines and in torments, and slavery; the sick and possessed; Christians in distress; toilers and servants; for fine weather, showers, dew, good fruits, and the harvest; (the Egyptian rites also pray for the due rise of the Nile); for those who labour in the churches; those who have offered to-day; fathers, patriarchs, prophets, apostles, martyrs, confessors, holy doctors, and all the righteous departed in the faith of Christ.

These subjects of intercession are much more extensive than those found in the Roman Solemn Prayers, and the following objects of intercession are not found in the Roman rite: the present congregation and the celebrant; the offerers (who are prayed for in the Roman rite in *Memento*, within the Canon); the weather; the rise of the Nile; the safety of man and beast; the founders of churches and monasteries; the faithful departed (who in the Roman rite are remembered in *Memento etiam* within the Canon); almsgivers and helpers of the poor and strangers; the city; the fruits of the earth; neophytes, slaves, eunuchs, ascetics, children, persecutors, married people, and child-bearing women.

On the other hand the Roman Solemn Prayers pray for Jews and pagans, heretics and schismatics, and the destruction of error, which are subjects not occurring in the Eastern rites, and, in common with the Eastern rites, they cover the most important classes of people to be prayed for: the whole Church and its peace; the bishop and all orders in the Church, and the whole people of God; rulers; catechumens; those suffering from disease, famine, imprisonment; travellers. The Roman intercessions are also much better arranged than the Eastern: they gather all the intercession together in one place in the rite, and do not repeat it with wearisome reiteration, two or three times; it is more succinct in expression, and it is not, as in many Eastern rites, left to the deacon and people while the celebrant carries on privately with his own prayers. It is shared by all: the deacon proclaims the bidding, calls for silent prayer, and after an interval for this the celebrant sums up the petitions in a collect.

St Augustine gives a good deal of evidence for the Prayer of the Faithful in Africa in the early fifth century. Immediately after the

[1] Brightman, *L.E.W.*, 54–6.

dismissal of the catechumens there was an act of intercession.[1] It included prayers for various classes of persons, for unbelievers, for the faithful, for the catechumens.[2] This common prayer (*communis oratio*) was called for by the deacon, who proclaimed the subjects of intercession in turn; and then the prayer was said by the bishop or the priest.[3] Evidently Africa used the same form of intercession as is seen in the *Orationes Sollemnes* of the Roman rite, now surviving only on Good Friday, in which the bishop or priest asks for prayers for various orders in the Church, and for other subjects of intercession, and then, after an interval of silent prayer, on their knees, the people are called upon to stand, and the bishop or priest says a collect.[4] We learn also from Augustine that this is a practically universal custom, and that it takes place in the mass before the Canon.[5] St Prosper of Aquitania, a little later than Augustine, traces the origin of the prayer of the faithful to apostolic times and says that it is universally offered all over the Church.[6] Writing about 432–4, he seems to have these intercessions

[1] Aug., *Serm.*, 49, 8; P.L. XXXVIII, 324; C.C. XLI, 620: ecce post sermonem fit missa catechumenis; manebunt fideles, uenietur ad locum orationis. *Ep.* 217, i, 2; P.L. XXXIII, 978; C.S.E.L. LVII, 404: exerce contra orationes ecclesiae disputationes tuas, et quando audis sacerdotem dei ad altare exhortantem populum dei orare pro incredulis, ut eos deus conuertat ad fidem; et pro catechumenis, ut eis desiderium regenerationis inspiret; et pro fidelibus, ut in eo quod esse coeperunt eius munere perseruerent . . . . *Ep.* 217, vii, 26; P.L. XXXIII, 988; C.S.E.L. LVII, 422: numquid, ubi audieris sacerdotem dei ad eius altare populum hortantem ad deum orandum uel ipsum clara uoce orantem, ut incredulas gentes ad fidem suam uenire compellat, non respondebis *Amen*?

[2] Aug., *De haer.*, 88; P.L. XLII, 48.

[3] Aug., *Ep.*, LV, xix, 34; P.L. XXXIII, 221; C.S.E.L. XXXIV, 209: quando autem non est tempus . . . sancta cantandi, nisi cum legitur aut disputatur aut antistites clara uoce deprecantur, aut communis oratio uoce diaconi indicitur?

[4] Caes. Arelat., *Serm.*, LXXVII; C.C. CIII, 319=Aug., *App. Serm.*, 286, 1: rogo et admoneo uos, fratres carissimi, ut quotienscumque iuxta altare a clericis oratur aut oratio diacono clamante indicitur, non solum corda sed etiam corpora fideliter inclinetis. nam dum frequenter sicut oportet et diligenter attendo, diacono clamante *Flectamus genua*, maximam partem uelut columnas erectas stare conspicio. Caes. Arelat., *Serm.*, LXXVI; C.C. CIII, 316=Aug., *App. Serm.*, 285, 1, P.L. XXXIX, 2284: ut quotienscumque oratio indicitur, qui forte pro aliqua infirmitate non potest genua flectere et dorsum curuare, et ceruicem humiliare non differat.

[5] Aug., *Ep.*, CXLIX, ii, 16; P.L. XXXIII, 637; C.S.E.L. XLIV, 362: eligo in his uerbis (*sc.* 1 Tim. 2. 1) hoc intelligere quod omnis uel paene omnis frequentat ecclesia, ut precationes accipiamus dictas, quas facimus in celebratione sacramentorum, antequam illud quod est in Domini mensa incipiat benedici; orationes cum benedicitur et sanctificatur et ad distribuendum comminuitur, quam totam petitionem fere omnis ecclesia dominica oratione concludit.

[6] Prosper, ap. Celestinum, *Ep. ad episcopos Galliae*, 11: ab apostolis traditae in toto mundo atque in omni ecclesia catholica uniformiter celebrantur.

in mind when he speaks of a universal custom of prayer for all men,[1] and in particular of prayer for the enemies of the Church and for unbelievers.[2] This evidence comes from a period when Prosper worked in southern Gaul, in Provence near Marseilles, where he stayed till about 435. He then moved to Rome, and there, between 435 and 442, he again refers to the universality of these general prayers of intercession.[3] Later still, about 450, he says that this practice is world-wide.[4] It has been shown by Dom Cappuyns that the *Capitula Auctoritatum* and the *De uocatione omnium gentium* are authentic works of Prosper of Aquitania.[5]

The *Oratio Fidelium* survived in this place in the mass, at the beginning of the Mass of the Faithful, in Gaul until the sixth century, for in 517 the Council of Lyon authorized one Stephen to remain in church until the prayer of the people, which was said after the Gospel.[6] At Rome there appears to be no mention of such prayers in this position after Felix III, who was Pope from 483 to 492. He prohibited a special category of penitents from being present at the prayers of the catechumens, let alone at the prayers of the faithful.[7]

It is clear from these and other pieces of evidence from all over the Church, from East as well as West, that in the first five centuries there was a general intercession in the mass. It included prayers for the Church, and for various orders and classes in the Church; the clergy, the people, the catechumens; for the sick and suffering, prisoners, travellers, and so forth; for penitents and for the lapsed; for kings and rulers; for the conversion of the heathen: in fact it constituted a general intercession for the Church and the world. It is evident that it formed usually in the East and always in the West part of the Mass of the

[1] Prosper, *Responsiones ad capitula obiectionum Vincentianarum*, 2; P.L. LI, 179 B: Apostolus . . . sollicitissime praecipit, quod in omnibus ecclesiis piissime custoditur, ut Deo pro omnibus hominibus supplicetur.

[2] Prosper, *Contra Collatorem*, 12, 3; P.L. LI, 245 B: ecclesia quotidie pro inimicis suis orat, id est pro his qui necdum Deo crediderunt.

[3] Prosper, *Capitula*, 8; P.L. LI, 209 C: in toto mundo atque in omni catholica ecclesia uniformiter celebrantur.

[4] Prosper, *De uocatione omnium gentium*, I, 12; P.L. LI, 664 C: nulla pars mundi . . . in qua huiusmodi orationes non celebrentur a populis christianis.

[5] M. Cappuyns, "Les *Orationes Sollemnes* du vendredi saint", in *Les Questions liturgiques et paroissiales*, 23, pp. 18–31; "L'auteur du *De Vocatione Omnium Gentium*", in *R.B.*, 39 (1927), pp. 198–226; "L'origine des *Capitula* pseudo-célestiens contre le semi-pélagianisme", in *R.B.*, 41 (1929), pp. 156–70.

[6] Mansi, *Sacrorum Conciliorum noua et amplissima collectio*, VIII, 570 B: usque ad orationem plebis quae post euangelia legeretur.

[7] Felix III, *Ep.* 7; P.L. LVIII, 925 C: nec orationi non modo fidelium sed ne catechumenorum omnimodis interesse.

Faithful, and not of the Mass of the Catechumens, and that it came after the Gospel. This implies that it began the Mass of the Faithful, for we read that it came before the Offertory and the Anaphora.

The position of the intercessory prayers is interesting in comparison with what we know of the synagogue worship of the Jews in early Christian times. The Mass of the Catechumens, with its scripture readings and psalms, seems to have some relation to synagogue worship. But in the synagogue worship the prayers came at the beginning, before the scripture readings. The following scheme shows the synagogue order:[1]

1. The offering of prayer (the *Shema*, certain benedictions, prayer).
2. The *Tephillah* (or *Shemoneh Esreh*, i.e. the eighteen Benedictions).
3. The reading of the Law (*Torah*).
4. The reading of the Prophets (the *Haphtarah*, i.e. conclusion).
5. Sermon or exhortation.
6. The offering of praise.
7. A psalm (probably).
8. The Aaronic blessing.

The reading of lessons from the scriptures has descended into the Christian service, and they are arranged in a definite order, in the case of the mass in an ascending order of importance, Old Testament, Epistle, Gospel, which is the opposite of the Jewish descending order, Law and then Prophets. But the intercession, which begins the synagogue office, has been moved from this position, and indeed out of the preliminary service, the Mass of the Catechumens, into the Mass of the Faithful.

Several authors describe the general intercession in the mass as an universal, or almost universal, custom; and in several places it is traced back in principle to the apostolic injunction of 1 Timothy 2. 1, 2: "I exhort, therefore, first of all, that supplications, prayers, intercessions, thanksgivings, be made for all men; for kings and all that are in high place; that we may lead a tranquil and quiet life in all godliness and gravity." The *Oratio Fidelium* does in fact fulfil this command, in

[1] Benedict Steuart, *The Development of Christian Worship*, London, 1953, pp. 8–9; C. W. Dugmore, *The influence of the Synagogue upon the Divine Office*, Oxford, 1944, pp. 11 ff.; J. Elbogen, *Studien zur Geschichte des jüdischen Gottesdienstes* (*Schriften der Lehranstalt für die Wissenschaft des Judenthums*, Band I, Heft 1, 2), Berlin, 1907.

praying for rulers, and for mankind in general; and it goes further, in praying for various other classes of people. It appears clearly for the first time in St Justin Martyr, and it was quite possibly, though not demonstrably, a feature of the Eucharist from apostolic days. All the indications in the first five centuries point to the same position in the rite, namely at the beginning of the Mass of the Faithful.

2. *The Intercessions of the Roman Mass*

A. ORATIONES SOLLEMNES

The present Roman *Ordo Missae* has no general block of intercession between the Gospel and the Offertory. But if we look at the order of Good Friday, we notice that in several respects it differs from the *Ordo Missae* on other days in the year. It is an afternoon mass, said after None, and its first rubric states that the priest and his assistants come to the altar and pray there silently for a space. Then a cloth is spread on the altar, and the priest comes to the altar and kisses it, and the mass begins immediately with the reading of the lessons, to which there is no introduction. This is the primitive beginning, which was lost by about the fifth century at Rome. There are, in the ancient manner, three lessons, the first two from the Old Testament, and the third the Gospel, which is the Passion according to St John. The Prophecy is divided from the second Old Testament lesson by a Tract and Collect (*Deus a quo et Iudas*), and this lesson from the Gospel by another Tract. The Gospel is immediately followed by the nine Solemn Prayers (*Orationes Sollemnes*), as they are entitled in the eighth century Sacramentaries and *Ordines*, and from that time onwards. There follow the Veneration of the Cross and the Reproaches, and the rite concludes with the priest's communion from the Reserved Sacrament.

This order comes down from primitive times. The Veneration of the Cross and the Reproaches are proper to Good Friday; the Communion from the Reserved Sacrament is an ancient practice once used on all aliturgical days; but the way in which the Mass begins straight away with the Lessons, the presence of three Lessons, and the solemn Intercessions after the Gospel, have nothing to do with Good Friday, but are simply a conservative retention of ancient practices once forming a regular feature of the Roman Mass.

The text of the Solemn Prayers cannot be traced back earlier than the eighth century, but there is no doubt that until the end of the fifth century they were a regular part of the order of the Roman mass.[1] The references quoted in Chapter I to the general intercession all fit these prayers, or prayers very similar to these, said at this point in the mass, after the Gospel.

The most ancient manuscripts which contain the Solemn Prayers are all of the eighth century, or the beginning of the ninth. The text here printed is derived from these, the oldest witnesses, which are representative of three distinct liturgical traditions, the Gelasian, the Gallican, and the Gregorian. Their substantial agreement shows that the form of the Solemn Prayers, with a bidding in each case, and a collect, is ancient, and goes back to the time before these three traditions diverged; and also that much of the actual text of the biddings and collects was settled at a similarly early date. On the other hand the three traditions diverge in certain respects, and particularly in the second and fourth of the prayers, those for the hierarchy and the civil authorities. The variants reflect different historical situations in these respects, and thus betray revisions on more than one occasion during the transmission of the prayers between, say, the fourth and the eighth centuries. These differences will be discussed in greater detail in Chapter III, but at this point it may be said, in anticipation, that none of the three traditions gives throughout what is likely to be the earliest form of the text. In view of this, it has not been thought wise to print as the standard the text of any one manuscript, but the text given on pages 14 ff. is an eclectic text, seeking to give the earliest available form of the Prayers.

For instance, after the *Oremus* before the Collect, the Gelasian manuscripts VRA give, in all nine cases, a rubric mentioning the diaconal proclamation, *Flectamus genua*, and *Leuate*. The St Gall manuscript of the Gelasian (S) gives a slightly different form of this direction in the first case, a reduced form in the second case, and subsequently no direction at all. The Gregorian manuscript O gives a full direction in the case of the first Prayer, and omits it subsequently. The older Gregorian manuscript C, and the *Missale Gallicanum Vetus*, omit any rubric. It seems probable that the last is the earliest form, because a

[1] See J. A. Jungmann, *The Early Liturgy to the Time of Gregory the Great*, London, 1960, p. 291.

rubric is inserted when people are forgetting how to perform a rite. When they know how a rite works, they do not need a rubric, and originally, when the Solemn Prayers were in daily use, no rubric would be necessary, as the practice would be familiar. By the sixth century these prayers were out of daily use, and only occurred in Holy Week, and therefore became comparatively unfamiliar; the necessity accordingly arose of having a rubric to tell people how to perform them, especially as the form of prayer with a bidding, a period of silent prayer, concluded by a collect, was an old-fashioned form which was going out of use. Thus it seems reasonable to conclude that the form without these rubrics (and without the rubrics at the beginning and end of this set of prayers) is the earliest form available.

The most ancient form of the Gelasian Sacramentary is to be found in the manuscript *Vaticanus Reginensis 316* (V), which was written in Gaul in the middle of the eighth century, about 750, in the region of Paris, probably for the convent of Chelles.[1] It certainly has Gallican additions and is not a purely Roman book, but its basis is Roman use of a much earlier period than the date of the manuscript. Its title is *In nomine Domini nostri Iesu Christi saluatoris incipit Liber Sacramentorum Romanae Ecclesiae ordinis anni circuli*, and Professor Chavasse has demonstrated that it is not a papal book, but a presbyteral sacramentary designed originally for use in the *tituli* of the city of Rome.[2] The presbyteral and Roman character of this sacramentary is particularly clear in the rites of the last three days of Holy Week, which include, of course, the Solemn Prayers of Good Friday.[3] The form in this sacramentary is that used in the Roman *tituli* in the latter half of the seventh century.

V, although it has later additions, is nearer to the primitive base than the eighth-century Gelasians. Three of these, which are scarcely less ancient than the Vatican *Reginensis* 316, are used in the construction of the text. They are *Rheinaugiensis* 30 (R), now at Zürich, which is of the eighth century; *Sangallensis* 348 (S), of about 800; and the Sacramentary of Angoulême (A), Paris, Bibliothèque Nationale, ms. Lat. 816, which was written at the end of the eighth or beginning of the ninth century.[4]

[1] E. A. Lowe, *Codices Latini Antiquiores*, VI, xxi–xxii, Oxford, 1953.

[2] A. Chavasse, *Le sacramentaire gélasien* (*Vaticanus Reginensis 316*): *Sacramentaire presbytérale en usage dans les titres romains au VIIe siècle*, Paris, 1958.

[3] A. Chavasse, *Le sacramentaire gélasien*, pp. 87–96, 634–5.

[4] The readings of *Reginensis* 316 are taken from L. C. Mohlberg, *Liber Sacramentorum Romanae Aeclesiae Ordinis anni circuli* (Cod. Vat. Reg. 316/Paris Bibl.

The text from the Gregorian Sacramentary in its oldest form is cited from the manuscripts *Cameracensis* 164 (159) at Cambrai, written in the year 812, and *Vaticanus Ottobonianus* 313 of the ninth century.[1]

The oldest text of the Solemn Prayers is not, however, that of the oldest manuscript of the Gelasian Sacramentary, but that found in *Missale Gallicanum Vetus*, where it is not derived from the *Gelasianum* or the *Gregorianum*, but from a more ancient Roman witness, which reached Gaul before the arrival of either of them, and represents a line of descent independent of the Gregorian and the Gelasian Sacramentaries.[2]

MANUSCRIPTS

Gelasian. (Gel.)

V Vaticanus Reginensis 316. c. 750.
R Rheinaugiensis 30. s. viii.
S Sangallensis 348. c. 800.
A Angoulême Sacramentary. Paris B.N. Lat. 816. c. 800.

Old Gallican (Gall.)

Missale Gallicanum Vetus, ed. L. C. Mohlberg, Rome, 1958 (*Rerum Ecclesiasticarum Documenta*, Fontes, 3). s. viii.

Gregorian. (Greg.)

C Cameracensis 164 (159). a. 812.
O Vaticanus Ottobonianus 313. s. ix.

Nat. 7193, 41/56) *Sacramentarium Gelasianum*, Rerum Ecclesiasticarum Documenta, Series Maior, Fontes, IV, Rome, 1960; of *Rheinaugiensis* 30 from H. A. Wilson, *The Gelasian Sacramentary*, Oxford, 1894; of *Sangallensis* 348 from D. Kunibert Mohlberg, *Das fränkische Sacramentarium Gelasianum in alamannischer Überliferung* (Codex Sangallensis No. 348), Münster-in-Westfalen, 1939 (*Liturgiegeschichtliche Quellen*, Heft 1/2); of the Angoulême Sacramentary from P. Cagin, *Le sacramentaire gélasien d'Angoulême*, Angoulême, 1918.

[1] Ed. Hans Lietzmann, *Das Sacramentarium Gregorianum nach dem Aachener Urexemplar*, Münster-in-Westfalen, 1921 (*Liturgiegeschichte Quellen*, 3).

[2] A. Chavasse, *Le sacramentaire gélasien*, pp. 634–5.

ITEM POST LECTIONEM EUANGELII ORATIONES SOLEMPNES

I

Oremus, dilectissimi nobis, in primis pro ecclesia sancta dei, ut eam deus et dominus noster pacificare adunare et custodire dignetur toto orbe
5 terrarum, subiciens ei principatus et potestates, detque nobis tranquillam et quietam uitam degentibus glorificare deum patrem omnipotentem.
Oremus. Omnipotens sempiterne deus, qui gloriam tuam omnibus in Christo gentibus reuelasti, custodi opera misericordiae tuae, ut ecclesia tua toto orbe diffusa stabili fide in confessione tui nominis perseueret.
10 per dominum nostrum.

II

Oremus et pro beatissimo papa nostro, ut deus omnipotens qui elegit eum in ordine episcopatus saluum et incolumem custodiat ecclesiae sanctae ad regendum populum sanctum dei.
Oremus. Omnipotens sempiterne deus, cuius aeterno iudicio uniuersa
15 fundantur, respice propitius ad preces nostras et electum nobis antistitem

1. ITEM POST LECTIONEM EUANGELII ORATIONES SOLEMPNES *Gall*: ITEM SECUNTUR ORATIONES SOLEMNES *Gel* (S); ORATIONES QUAE DICENDAE SUNT VI FERIA MAIORE IN HIERUSALEM *Greg*; Item sequitur lectio et responsorium (responsurium V). Inde uero legitur passio domini. Ipsa expleta incipit sacerdos (sacerdus V) orationes (oratio V) sollemnes (solempnes V, solemnes A) quae sequuntur (secuntur A) *Gel* (VRA). 3. in primis *om. Greg*. eclesia *Gel* (S). eam: etiam *Gel* (V). 4. adunare: multiplicare *Gall*; *om. Greg* (C). toto orbe *Gall Gel* (RS) *Greg* (C): per uniuersum orbem *Gel* (VA) *Greg* (O). 5. potestatis *Gall*. 6. >quietam et tranquillam *Greg*. quietem *Gel* (VA). 7. OREMUS+*Et dicit diaconos*. Flectamus genua. *Postquam orauerint dicit* Leuate. *Gel*. (S); +*Adnuntiat diaconus*, Flectamus genua. *Iterum dicit*, Leuate. *Gel* (VRA) *Greg* (O); *deinde*+postea dicit sacerdos orationem *Greg* (O). Adnuntiat: et dicit *Gel* (S) *Greg* (O); et adnunciat *Gel* (A). Iterum: postquam orauerint *Gel* (S) *Greg* (O); et iterum *Gel* (A). sempiternae *Gall*. tuam+in *Gel* (V). 8. aecclesia *Gel* (V), ecclea *Gel* (S). 9. tua *om. Gall. Greg* (C). stabile *Gall*. confessionem *Gel* (V) *Greg* (C) *Gall*. 10. per dominum nostrum *Gall Greg*: per *Gel* (RA); per dominum *Gel* (V); per eundem dominum nostrum Iesum *Gel* (S). 11. beatissimo: famulo dei *Gel* (VA). nostro+ille *Gel* (S); +illo *Greg*; +sedis apostolicae illo *Gel* (VRA); *deinde*+et pro antistite (antestite VA) nostro *Illo Gel* (VRA). omnipotens: et dominus noster *Greg*. 11–12. qui . . . episcopatus *sup. lin.* A[c]; *post* sanctae *ponit* A* (ordinatione episcopatus). eum: eos *Gel* (VRA). 12. ordinem *Greg*. saluum: saluos *Gel* (VRA). et: atque *Greg*. incolumem *Greg* (C): incolomem *Gall Greg* (O) *Gel* (S); incolumes *Gel* (VRA). ecclesiae+suae *Gel Greg*. 14. OREMUS+Item adnuntiat (-ciat A) diaconus ut supra *Gel* (VRA); +diaconus ut supra *Gel* (S). aeterno *om. Greg*. iudicio: inditio *Gall*. 15. propicius *Gel* (VS). praeces *Gall Gel* (VSA). electum . . . antistitem *Greg*: electum . . . antestitem *Gall Gel* (S); electos . . . antistites *Gel* (R); electos . . .

tua pietate conserua, ut christiana plebs quae tali gubernatur auctore sub tanto pontifice credulitatis suae meritis augeatur. per.

III

Oremus et pro omnibus episcopis, presbyteris, diaconibus, subdiaconibus, acolytis, exorcistis, lectoribus, ostiariis, confessoribus, uirginibus, uiduis,
20 et pro omni populo sancto dei.

OREMUS. Omnipotens sempiterne deus, cuius spiritu totum corpus ecclesiae sanctificatur et regitur, exaudi nos pro uniuersis ordinibus supplicantes, ut gratiae tuae munere ab omnibus tibi gradibus fideliter seruiatur. per.

IV

25 Oremus et pro christianissimis imperatoribus nostris ut deus et dominus noster subditas illis faciat omnes barbaras nationes ad nostram perpetuam pacem. per.

OREMUS. Omnipotens sempiterne deus, in cuius manu sunt omnium temporum potestates et omnia iura regnorum, respice propitius ad
30 Romanum benignus imperium, ut gentes quae in sua feritate confidunt potentiae tuae dextera conprimantur. per.

V

Oremus et pro catechumenis nostris, ut deus et dominus noster adaperiat

antestites *Gel* (VA). electum (*uel* electos)+a te *Gel*. 16. que *Gall*. tali . . . auctore: talibus . . . auctoribus *Gel* (VRA). gobernatur *Gel* (S). 17. tanto pontifice *Gall Greg*: tanto pontefice *Gel* (S); tantis pontificibus *Gel* (RA); tantos pontifices *Gel* (V). meretis *Gall*. per+dominum nostrum Iesum *Gel* (S); +dnm *Greg*. 18. praesbyteris *Gel* (V); prebiteris *Gel* (S); prstris *Gel* (A); praesbiteris *Gall*; presbiteris *Greg* (O). subdiaconibus *om. Gall*. 19. acolitis *Gel* (SA) *Gall Greg* (O); acolothis *Greg* (C). hostiariis *Gel* (V). uirgenibus *Gel* (V). 21. OREMUS+Item adnuntiat (-ciat A) diaconus ut supra Gel (VRA). 23. munera *Gall*; munerae *Gel* (S*). tibi gradibus *om. Gel* (V). seruiantur *Gel* (A). 24. per+dominum *Gel* (A) *Gall Greg* (O); +dominum nostrum *Greg* (C); +dominum nostrum Iesum Christum *Gel* (S*); *deinde*+in unitate eiusdem *Gel* (S^c). 25. christianissimis imperatoribus nostris *Gel* (S): christianissimo imperatore nostro *Greg*; christianissimis imperatoribus nostris uel rege nostro *Ill. Gel* (R); christianissimo imperatore nostro uel rege nostro *Illo Gel* (V); christianissimo imperatore uel rege nostro *illo Gel* (A); christianissimis regibus *Gall*. 25–6. et dominus noster: omnipotens *Gel* (VA). 26. illis: illi *Greg*. 27. per *om. Gel Greg*. 28. OREMUS+Item adnuntiat (-ciat A) diaconus ut supra *Gel* (VRA). 28–9. in cuius manu (manum *Gall*; manus *Greg* C) sunt omnium temporum (temporum *om. Greg*) potestates et omnia iura regnorum *Gall Greg*: qui regnis omnibus aeterna potestate dominaris *Gel*. 29. propicius *Gel* (VS); *om. Greg*. 30. Romanum *Gall Gel* (VA) *Greg* (C); romanorum *Gel* (RS); christianum *Greg* (O); +siue Francorum *Gel* (VA); +atque Francorum *Gel* (R). 31. potentiae tuae dextera *Gall Greg Gel* (RS); dexterae tuae potentia *Gel* (V); dexterae potentia *Gel* (A*); dexterae maiestatis tuae potentia *Gel* (A^e). conprimantur *Gel* (VRA); comprimantur *Greg*; conpraemantur *Gall Gel* (S). per+dnm *Greg* (C); +dnm nrm *Gel* (A). 32. caticuminis *Gel* (VSA); catacuminis *Gall*; catecuminis *Greg* (O).

aures praecordiarum ipsorum ianuamque misericordiae, ut per lauacrum regenerationis accepta remissione omnium peccatorum digni inueniantur
35 in Christo Iesu domino nostro.

OREMUS. Omnipotens sempiterne deus, qui ecclesiam tuam noua semper prole fecundas, auge fidem et intellectum catechumenis nostris, ut renati fonte baptismatis adoptionis tuae filiis adgregentur. per.

VI

Oremus, dilectissimi nobis, deum patrem omnipotentem ut cunctis
40 mundum purget erroribus, morbos auferat, famem depellat, aperiat carceres, uincula dissoluat, peregrinantibus reditum, infirmantibus sanitatem, nauigantibus portum salutis indulgeat.

OREMUS. Omnipotens sempiterne deus, maestorum consolatio, laborantium fortitudo, perueniant ad te preces de quacumque tribulatione
45 clamantium, ut omnes sibi in necessitatibus suis misericordiam tuam gaudeant adfuisse. per.

VII

Oremus et pro hereticis et schismaticis, ut deus et dominus noster eruat eos ab erroribus uniuersis et ad sanctam matrem ecclesiam catholicam atque apostolicam reuocare dignetur. per.

50 OREMUS. Omnipotens sempiterne deus, qui omnes saluas et neminem uis perire, respice ad animas diabolica fraude deceptas, ut omni heretica prauitate deposita errantium corda resipiscant et ad ueritatis tuae redeant firmitatem. per.

VIII

Oremus et pro perfidis iudaeis, ut deus et dominus noster auferat uelamen

33. precordiarum *Gel* (A); precordiorum *Gel* (S). ipsorum: eorum *Gel* (RS[c]). ianuamque: genuamque *Gel* (V). 34. regenerationes *Gall.* acceptam remissionem *Gel* (A); accepta remissionem *Gel* (V). digni: et ipsi *Gall Greg.* 36. OREMUS+Adnuntiat (item adnunciat A) diaconus ut supra *Gel* (VRA). aeclesiam *Gel* (V). nouam *Gall.* 37. caticuminis *Gel* (VSA); catecumenis *Gall Greg* (O). 38. babtismatis *Gel* (S*). tuae: tuem *Gel* (A). aggregentur *Gel* (R) *Greg.* per+dominum *Gel* (S) *Gall Greg*; +dn̄m nr̄m *Gel* (A). 41. carceris *Gall.* uincola *Gel* (S*); uincla *Gel* (S[c]) *Gall. Greg* (C). 43. OREMUS+Adnuntiat (item adnunciat A) diaconus ut supra *Gel* (VRA). sempiterne: et misericors *Gel* (S) *Gall.* moestorum *Gel* (R); mestorum *Gel* (S) *Gall.* laborancium *Gel* (A). 44. praeces *Gel* (V) *Gall.* 46. per+dominum *Gall Gel* (VR); +dominum nostrum Iesum *Gel* (S). 47. et (*pr.*) *om. Gel* (SA* +et *post* pro A[c]) *Gall.* heredicis *Gel* (V) *Gall*; haereticis *Gel* (R) *Greg.* scismaticis *Gel* (VSA) *Gall Greg.* et (*tert.*): ac *Gel* (RS) *Gall Greg.* 48. ad *om. Gall* (*lapsu*). aeclesiam *Gel* (V). 49. per *om. Gel* (RSA) *Greg*; +dominum *Gall.* 50. OREMUS+Adnuntiat (adnunciat V; item adnunciat A) diaconus ut supra Gel (VRA). >saluas omnes *Gel* (RS) *Gall Greg.* niminem *Gel* (V). 51. heredica *Gel* (V); haeretica *Gel* (RS) *Greg.* 52. prauitate: peruersitate *Gel* (VA). deposita: depulsa *Gel* (VRA); +et *Gel* (S). errancium *Gel* (V). errantium corda *om. Gall.* 53. firmitatem: unitatem *Greg.* per+dominum *Gel* (VRS) *Greg* (C); +dn̄m nr̄m *Gel* (A). 54. iudeis *Gel* (S).

55 de cordibus eorum, ut et ipsi cognoscant Christum Iesum dominum nostrum.

OREMUS. Omnipotens sempiterne deus, qui etiam iudaicam perfidiam a tua misericordia non repellis, exaudi preces nostras, quas tibi pro illius populi obcaecatione deferimus, ut agnita ueritatis tuae luce, quae Christus
60 est, a suis tenebris eruantur. per.

IX

Oremus et pro paganis, ut deus omnipotens auferat iniquitatem a cordibus eorum, et relictis idolis suis conuertantur ad deum uerum et unicum filium eius Iesum Christum dominum nostrum, cum quo uiuit et regnat cum Spiritu sancto.

65 OREMUS. Omnipotens sempiterne deus, qui non mortem peccatorum sed uitam semper inquiris, suscipe propitius orationem nostram et libera eos ab idolorum cultura, et adgrega ecclesiae tuae sanctae ad laudem et gloriam nominis tui. per.

>dominus et deus *Gel* (S). 55. de: a *Greg* (O). cognuscant *Gel* (S). *Gall*; agnoscant *Greg*. >ihm xpm *Gel* (A) *Greg* (O). iesum *om. Gel* (S). 56. nostrum+qui uiuit et regnat *Gall.* 57. OREMUS+Adnuntiat (adnunciat V, item adnunciat A) diaconus ut supra *Gel* (VRA). iudaeicam *Gall.* a *om. Gall.* 58. misericordiam *Gel* (A). praece s *Gel* (V) *Gall.* tibi *om. Gall Greg.* 59. obcaecationem *Gel* (V); obcecatione *Gel* (S) *Gall.* agnita: cognita *Gel* (R). lucem *Gall*; lucae *Gel* (S*). que *Gall.* 60. per+dominum *Greg* (C) *Gel* (VR); eundem *Greg* (O); +dnm nrm *Gel* (SA). 61. iniquitates *Gel* (S); iniqua *Gall.* a: de *Gel* (S) *Gall.* 62. deum+uiuum et *Gel* (S) *Greg.* 63. Christum+deum ac *Gel* (S); +deum et *Greg* (C). dominum nostrum *om. Gall.* cum quo uiuit et regnat cum Spiritu sancto *om. Gel.* (A). cum quo: qui cum eo *Greg* (O). 64. cum Spiritu sancto *Gall Greg* (C); cum sancto Spiritu *Greg* (O); Deus in unitate spiritus sancti *Gel.* sancto+in saecula saeculorum *Gall*; +deus per omnia saecula saeculorum amen *Greg* (O) *Gel* (RS^c). 65. OREMUS+Adnuntiat (item adnunciat A) diaconus ut supra *Gel* (VRA). non+uis *Greg* (O). 66. propicius *Gel* (VS). 67. aggrega *Gel* (RS) *Greg* (C); adgrege *Gall.* ecclesiae: eclae *Gal* (S). 68. per+dominum nostrum iesum christum filium tuum, qui tecum uiuit et regnat deus in unitate spiritus sancti per omnia secula seculorum Amen *Gel* (S); +per dominum nostrum Iesum Christum filium tuum, qui uiuit et regnat in saecula saeculorum *Gall. deinde*+Istas orationes supra (super A) scriptas expletas, ingrediuntur diaconi in sacrario (+et A). Procedunt cum corpore et sanguine (sanguinis V) Domini qui ante die (diem A) remansit, et ponunt super altare. Et uenit sacerdos ante altare adorans crucem Domini et osculans. Et dicit *Oremus.* Et sequitur. *Praeceptis* (preceptis A) *salutaribus moniti* et oratio dominica. Inde *Libera nos domine quaesumus* (>qs dne A). Haec omnia expleta (expleti R) adorant omnes sanctam crucem et communicant. *Gel* (VRA).

The *Ordines Romani* contain descriptions of the performance of the *Orationes Sollemnes* between the eighth and the tenth centuries. The earliest *Ordo* to refer to them is *Ordo* XXIII, which is perhaps of the early eighth century, and in that case a little earlier than the earliest text of the Solemn Prayers in a sacramentary, which is that of the Gelasian *Codex Vaticanus Reginensis* 316, of about 750. *Ordo* XXIII, 20 describes the Papal liturgy at St John's on Good Friday, in which, after the Passion has been read, the Pope says, "Oremus pro aeclesia sancta dei", and the archdeacon, "Flectamus genua", and afterwards, "Leuate".[1]

Ordo XXIV contains the office for Holy Week. It is not a papal rite from Rome, but designed for a bishop, attended by priests, deacons, subdeacons, and acolytes; and, though it was probably composed in Frankish territory, it is Roman and not Gallican, and the author was evidently familiar with Roman usage. Its date is the second half of the eighth century. It first describes the Solemn Prayers as being said on Wednesday before Easter,[2] when the prayers were performed as an office separate from the mass, and taking place about 9 in the morning, whereas the mass on this day was said at 2 p.m.[3] This is the earliest *ordo* to mention their recital on the Wednesday and apart from mass, and the other orders which mention these facts derive from this *Ordo* XXIV.[4] Amalarius refers also to the use of these prayers on Wednesday.[5] The bishop omits the prayer for himself,[6] and after the prayer for the Roman Emperor he adds one for the King of the Franks.[7] The genuflexion is omitted at the eighth prayer, for the Jews.[8] This omission is mentioned in other *ordines*, but this appears to be the earliest mention of it, and the rubrics of the sacramentaries contain no reference to it. At the end of the Solemn Prayers the bishop kisses the altar and departs,[9] and returns at 2 p.m. to celebrate mass.[10] On Good Friday the Prayers come in their normal place in the liturgy, after the Gospel.[11]

Ordo XXVII comes from the second half of the eighth century, and incorporates material from *Ordo* XXIV. It states that the bishop, attended by all the clergy from the city and the suburbs, performs the Solemn Prayers on Wednesday morning according to the text of the Sacramentary.[12] As in *Ordo* XXIV, the prayers are said in the usual form, and the bishop omits the prayer for himself, and the genuflexion

[1] M. Andrieu, *Les Ordines Romani du haut moyen âge*, III, *Spicilegium Sacrum Lovaniense*, 24, Louvain, 1951, pp. 271–2.

[2] XXIV, 1; Andrieu, op. cit., III, p. 287.

[3] XXIV, 5.

[4] Namely *Ordines* XXVII, 14–15; XXVIII, 4; XXIX, 4; XXXI, 4–5; L, xxiv, 3.

[5] Amalarius, *De eccles. officiis*, I, xi, 1; P.L. CV, 1009 A, ed. Hanssens, II, 60.

[6] XXIV, 2; Andrieu, op. cit., III, p. 288.

[7] Ibid., XXIV, 3.

[8] Ibid., XXIV, 3.

[9] XXIV, 4.

[10] XXIV, 5.

[11] XXIV, 26–7; Andrieu, op. cit., III, p. 293.

[12] XXVII, 14; Andrieu, op. cit., III, p. 351.

is omitted at the eighth prayer, for the Jews.[1] The mass is said at 2 p.m. as a separate service.[2]

Ordo XXX B, of the end of the eighth century, says that the priest on Good Friday says the Solemn Prayers after the Gospel.[3] In *Ordo* XXVIII, a Frankish *ordo* of about 800, the bishop says the Solemn Prayers before the altar on Wednesday and on Friday, and there is no genuflexion at the prayer for the Jews.[4] *Ordo* XXIX is mostly derived from XXVII, and is the work of a Frankish monk in the last quarter of the ninth century. It describes the Solemn Prayers on Wednesday,[5] when mass follows at 3 p.m.;[6] and on Friday.[7] There is no genuflexion at the prayer for the Jews.[8] *Ordo* XXXI, of a date earlier than 900, comes from Gaul, and provides for the Solemn Prayers on Wednesday,[9] and on Friday.[10] It notes that the bishop omits the prayer for himself, and the genuflexion at the prayer for the Jews. *Ordo* XXXII prescribes the Solemn Prayers on Good Friday.[11] The latest of the *Ordines* to mention the Prayers is *Ordo* L, dating from about 950, which prescribes them on Wednesday, with an extra prayer for the King of the Franks after the prayer for the Emperor, and with the omission of the genuflexion at the prayer for the Jews.[12] Under Good Friday some of the manuscripts of this *Ordo* which date from the eleventh and twelfth centuries give the actual text of the Solemn Prayers.[13] R (Rheinau 30, 8th–9th century) is the only Antiphonary which notes their recital on Good Friday.[14]

B. DEPRECATIO GELASII

The Solemn Prayers, restricted to Holy Week since the end of the fifth century, were evidently an ancient feature of the Roman rite, and in daily use until that time. It is uncertain how soon they came to be used in their present form, but it seems likely that from the second

[1] XXVII, 15. [2] XXVII, 18; Andrieu, op. cit., III, p. 352.
[3] XXX B, 33; Andrieu, op. cit., III, p. 471.
[4] XXVIII, 35; Andrieu, op. cit., III, p. 399. [5] XXIX, 3–5. [6] XXIX, 6.
[7] XXIX, 33; Andrieu, op. cit., III, pp. 437, 442. [8] XXIX, 4.
[9] XXXI, 4; Andrieu, op. cit., III, p. 491.
[10] XXXI, 41; Andrieu, op. cit., III, p. 497.
[11] XXXII, 9; Andrieu, op. cit., III, p. 519.
[12] L, xxvii, 13; Andrieu, op. cit., V, p. 248. *Spicilegium Sacrum Lovaniense*, 29, Louvain, 1961.
[13] L, xxvii, 13; Andrieu, op. cit., V, pp. 248–52.
[14] Ed. Hesbert. No. 78. postea uero uadit Sacerdus ante altare et dicit *Oremus* et dicit *Leuate. Flectamus genua.*

century, from the time of Justin Martyr at least, there was a general intercession in the Roman mass after the Gospel. The last mention of this as a regular practice is, as we have seen,[1] by Pope Felix III (483–92). His successor was Gelasius, who was Pope for a very short period, 492–6. It seems certain that Gelasius in his short pontificate made some definite contribution to Roman worship. The notice in *Liber Pontificalis* concerning him says, "Fecit et sacramentorum praefationes et orationes cauto sermone".[2] As this was written only some thirty years after his death, it is likely to be correct, but it is not easy to be certain what precise liturgical changes are to be attributed to Gelasius. The *Sacramentarium Gelasianum* is not so termed in its own title, which in the earliest manuscript (*Vaticanus Reginensis* 316) is *Liber Sacramentorum Romanae Ecclesiae ordinis anni circuli*, and in other manuscripts *Liber Sacramentorum*, sometimes with the addition of *Romanae Ecclesiae*. And though Walafrid Strabo says of Gelasius, "tam a se quam ab aliis compositas preces dicitur ordinasse",[3] which might well describe the drafting of a sacramentary, consisting of older prayers and original compositions of the editor, this is only hearsay, and of a somewhat later date since this work was written in 841. Professor A. Chavasse has identified in the *Leonianum* a number of masses composed by Gelasius, and some more from the hand of Vigilius (537–55).[4] The style of these masses is careful and complicated, sometimes obscure, and similar as well to the writings and letters of Gelasius as to the carefully constructed *Deprecatio Gelasii*. After thorough consideration of the work of Gelasius in this field, Dom B. Capelle concludes that the Gelasian Sacramentary is not the work of Gelasius as a whole, but must be dated in the sixth century, between the death of Vigilius, who made a contribution to it, and the accession of St Gregory the Great, that is between 555 and 590.[5]

An *Ordo baptismi*, "*Ordo Romanus* VII",[6] dating back to the end of the

[1] P. 8, *supra*.
[2] *Liber Pontificalis*, ed. L. Duchesne, I, p. 255.
[3] *Libellus de exordiis et incrementis quarundam in obseruationibus ecclesiasticis rerum*, XXII; P.L. CXIV, 946 B; *Monumenta Germaniae Historica*, Legum Sectio II, *Capitularia Regum Francorum*, Tomi II, pars tertia, Appendix, p. 498, Hanover, 1897; ed. Knoepfler, Munich, 1890, p. 59.
[4] *Ephemerides Liturgicae*, 64, Rome, 1950, pp. 161–213; "Messes du pape Gélase dans le sacramentaire léonien", in *Rev. Bén.* 56, Maredsous 1945–6; pp. 12–41; "Retouches gélasiennes dans le sacramentaire léonien", in *Rev. Bén.*, 61 (1951), pp. 3–14.
[5] See B. Capelle, "L'oeuvre liturgique de s. Gélase", in *J.T.S.*, N.S. 2, Oxford, 1951, pp. 129–44; reprinted in *Travaux liturgiques*, II, 146–60.
[6] P.L. LXXVIII, 996.

sixth century, gives a detailed account of the mass. It mentions the Gospel, then the oblations, then the Secret. The absence of any mention of the *Oratio Fidelium* is significant. It would appear, therefore, that the Solemn Prayers disappeared from regular use during the sixth century.[1]

They appear to have been replaced by the *Deprecatio quam Papa Gelasius pro uniuersali ecclesia constituit canendam esse*. This is a Litany on an oriental pattern, to which the response of the people is *Kyrie eleison*. There is every reason to accept its title in the manuscripts as authentic, and to see in it an intercession introduced by Gelasius to replace the Solemn Prayers.[2] It was not, however, inserted in the same place as the Solemn Prayers, after the Gospel, but was placed before the beginning of the mass.[3] It is related to the Litany in the Stowe Missal,[4] and has similarities of style with the writings of Gelasius,[5] being written in a carefully constructed form.

The following text of the *Deprecatio Gelasii* is that printed by Dom Capelle, and is based on ms. Paris 1153, with readings of *Angelica* B.3.18 (=A).[6] It is, however, set out in the form suggested by C. Callewaert,[7] which distinguishes the deacon's part (e.g. "pro inmaculata dei uiui ecclesia per totum orbem constituta") from that of the *schola cantorum* ("*diuinae bonitatis opulentiam deprecamur*"), while the response *Kyrie eleison* belongs to the people.

[1] B. Capelle, "Le pape Gélase et la messe romaine", in *Rev. d'hist. ecclés.*, 35, Louvain, 1939, pp. 22–34; reprinted in *Travaux liturgiques*, II, 135–45.

[2] See B. Capelle, "L'oeuvre liturgique de s. Gélase", in *J.T.S.*, N.S. 2, Oxford, 1951, pp. 137–8; and *Travaux liturgiques*, II, 146–60. "Le pape Gélase et la messe romaine", in *Revue d'histoire ecclésiastique*, 35, Louvain, 1939, pp. 22–34; and *Travaux liturgiques*, II, 135–45.

[3] B. Capelle, "Le Kyrie de la messe et le pape Gélase", in *R.B.*, 46, pp. 126–44, Louvain, 1934; and *Travaux liturgiques*, II, 116–34.

[4] *R.B.* 46, p. 138; *Trav. lit.*, II, 128.

[5] *R.B.* 46, p. 141; *Trav. lit.*, II, 130–2

[6] *R.B.* 46, pp. 136–8; *Trav. lit.*, II, 126–8.

[7] C. Callewaert, "Les étapes de l'histoire du Kyrie: s. Gélase, s. Benoît, s. Grégoire", in *R.H.E.* 38, pp. 20–45, Louvain, 1942.

DEPRECATIO QUAM PAPA GELASIUS PRO UNIUERSALI ECCLESIA CONSTITUIT CANENDAM ESSE

a. Dicamus omnes: Domine exaudi et miserere

5 b. Patrem Unigeniti et Dei Filium Genitoris ingeniti et sanctum Deum Spiritum fidelibus animis inuocamus.

Kyrie eleison.

I. Pro inmaculata Dei uiui ecclesia per totum orbem constituta

diuinae bonitatis opulentiam deprecamur.

10 Kyrie eleison.

II. Pro sanctis Dei magni sacerdotibus et ministris sacri altaris cunctisque Deum uerum colentibus populis

Christum Dominum supplicamus.

Kyrie eleison.

15 III. Pro uniuersis recte tractantibus uerbum ueritatis

multiformem Verbi Dei sapientiam peculiariter obsecramus.

Kyrie eleison.

IV. Pro his qui se mente et corpore propter caelorum regna castificant, et spiritalium labore desudant

20 *largitorem spiritalium munerum obsecramus.*

Kyrie eleison.

V. Pro religiosis principibus omnique militia eorum, qui iustitiam et rectum iudicium diligunt

Domini potentiam obsecramus.

25 Kyrie eleison.

VI. Pro iocunditate serenitatis et opportunitate pluuiae atque aurarum uitalium blandimentis ac diuersorum temporum prospero cursu

rectorem mundi Dominum deprecamur.

Kyrie eleison.

4. Dicamus . . . miserere: Kyrie eleison A. 5. Patrem Unigeniti: Deum Patrem A. et . . . ingeniti: Filiumque eius Dnum Iesum Christum A. 5–6. sanctum Deum Spiritum: Spiritum sanctum A. 6. fidelibus: deuotis A. inuocemus A. 7. Kyrie eleison *om.* 1153 *hic et semper.* 8. inmaculata: catholica A. per . . . constituta: sacerdotibus ac ministris 1153. 9. diuinae bonitatis opulentiam: misericordem dominum A. deprecemur A. 11. sanctis Dei magni *om.* A. sacri altaris *om.* 1153. cunctisque: et cunctis A. 13. Christum Dominum supplicamus: Domini potentiam deprecemur A. 22. Pro . . . eorum: Pro domno illo imperatore nostro, iudicibus et exercitibus eius A. 22–3. iustitiam . . . iudicium: iudicium et iustitiam 1153. 24. Domini potentiam obsecramus: misericordem Dominum deprecemur A. 26. serenitatis . . . pluuiae: et serenitate pluuiae

30 VII. Pro his quos prima christiani nominis initiauit agnitio, quos iam desiderium gratiae caelestis accendit
omnipotentis Dei misericordiam obsecramus.
Kyrie eleison.

VIII. Pro his quos humanae infirmitatis fragilitas, et quos nequitiae
35 spiritalis inuidia uel uarius saeculi error inuoluit
Redemptoris nostri misericordiam imploramus.
Kyrie eleison.

IX. Pro his quos peregrinationis necessitas aut iniquae potestatis oppressio uel hostilitatis uexat aerumna
40 *Saluatorem Dominum supplicamus.*
Kyrie eleison.

X. Pro iudaica falsitate . . . aut heretica prauitate deceptis uel gentilium superstitione perfusis
ueritatis Dominum deprecemur.
45 Kyrie eleison.

XI. Pro operariis pietatis et his qui necessitatibus laborantum fraterna caritate subueniunt
misericordiarum Dominum deprecamur.
Kyrie eleison.

50 XII. Pro omnibus intrantibus in haec sanctae domus Domini atria . . . religioso corde et supplici deuotione conuenerunt
Dominum gloriae deprecamur.
Kyrie eleison.

XIII. Pro emundatione animarum corporumque nostrorum et omnium
55 uenia peccatorum
clementissimum Dominum supplicamus.
Kyrie eleison.

XIV. Pro refrigerio fidelium animarum praecipue sanctorum Domini sacerdotum, qui huic ecclesiae praefuerunt catholicae
60 *Dominum spirituum et uniuersae carnis iudicem deprecamur.*
Kyrie eleison.

XV. Mortificatam uitiis carnem et uiuentem fide animam
praesta, Domine, praesta.

1153. aurarum: orarum 1153. 27. diuersorum temporum prospero: prospero diuersorum operum 1153. 28. rectorem . . . deprecamur: omnipotentem Dominum supplicemus A. 35. error: horror 1153. 38. oppressio: impietas 1153. 39. hostilitatis: hostilis 1153. 40. saluatorem Dominum supplicamus: conditoris nostri misericordiam deprecemur A. 42. *post* falsitate *lacunam unius uerbi hic suspicor*-Capelle. 50. *post* atria: *aliquid hic deest forte* qui . . . *uel melius* ibique. 54. et omnium: omnium ac 1153. 56. clementissimum: conditorem mundi A. supplicemus A. 58. refrigerio: requie A. 59. catholicae *om.* A. 60. deprecamur:

XVI. Castum timorem et ueram dilectionem
65 *praesta, Domine, praesta.*
XVII. Gratum uitae ordinem et probabilem exitum
praesta, Domine, praesta.
XVIII. Angelum pacis et solacia sanctorum
praesta, Domine, praesta.
70 Nosmetipsos et omnia nostra quae orta quae aucta per Dominum
ipso auctore suscipimus
ipso custode retinemus
ipsiusque misericordiae et arbitrio
prouidentiae commendamus.
75 Domine miserere.

supplicemus A. 70–5. nosmetipsos . . . miserere: Exaudi Domine uocem famuli tui pro incolumitate po/A (*cetera desunt*). 70. aucta: *cod. habet* acta, *forte recte.* 73. ipsiusque: *perperam delet* que MEYER.

The *Deprecatio Gelasii* is not modelled upon the *Orationes Sollemnes* in structure, subjects of intercession, or language. But it does in fact include all the persons or classes prayed for in the Solemn Prayers, and contains other intercessions not mentioned in the Solemn Prayers, for example, one for the departed. The following table will show the fact that the two schemes of intercession cover the same ground.

Orationes Sollemnes	*Subject*	*Deprecatio Gelasii*
I	The Church	I
II	The Pope, the Bishop, and the People	II
III	Orders in the Church	II, III, IV
IV	Emperor (or King)	V
V	Catechumens	VII(?)
VI	Those in error or tribulation	VIII, IX, X
VII	Heretics and schismatics	X
VIII	Jews	X[1]
IX	Pagans and idolaters	X

The Solemn Prayers disappeared from the regular liturgy at Rome under Pope Gelasius, between 492 and 496, and remained only on Good Friday, on which day they have continued to be used down to the present time. They were replaced by the *Deprecatio Gelasii* said

[1] It is not clear whether the *Deprecatio* prays for the Jews. As it stands in the manuscripts it asks for prayer for those deceived by Jewish perfidy and heretical depravity, but Dom Capelle suspects a lacuna of one word after *falsitate*, and, if this is the case, it might refer to persons implicated in Jewish perfidy, or else to the victims of such perfidy; it is not possible to conjecture what the missing word was.

before mass. But this Litany in its turn disappeared, evidently not later than St Gregory the Great, a century later than Gelasius (590–604). It left its mark on the mass, however, in the form of its response, *Kyrie eleison*, which still stands in the same position at the beginning of the mass, amplified since the sixth century by the addition of *Christe eleison*. St Gregory the Great, writing in 598 to John, Bishop of Syracuse, appears to refer to these changes when he says that the Romans do not use, and never have used, *Kyrie eleison* according to the Greek fashion; and also that in weekday masses something had been omitted, leaving *Kyrie eleison* and *Christe eleison*.[1] This can hardly be anything other than the *Deprecatio Gelasii*: if so, it had disappeared on weekdays in St Gregory's times, doubtless owing to its length, but was evidently retained on Sundays. It cannot have been long after that it vanished completely.

In the Ordinary of the Mass according to the present Roman rite there is after the Creed a puzzling *Dominus uobiscum*. R. *Et cum spiritu tuo*, after which the priest says *Oremus*. This is not, however, followed by a prayer. Immediately he says the offertory chant, if this is not sung. It is evident that some prayer must have dropped out at this point, leaving the Salutation and *Oremus* which used to precede it. Is it possible to identify the prayer which has disappeared? There seem to be three possibilities. (1) the *Orationes Sollemnes*; (2) the second Collect which appears in many masses of the Gelasian Sacramentary; (3) the Secret, or *Oratio super oblata*, which does not now follow immediately, but may well have done so before the offertory prayers and other material were inserted. All these three occurred after the Gospel or Sermon (and of course the Creed is a later addition), and it is possible that the *Oremus* may have originally belonged to any of the three, but liturgical scholars are much divided on the answer to this question.

1. Among those who think that this *Oremus* introduced the Solemn Prayers are F. E. Brightman,[2] A. Fortescue,[3] L. Duchesne,[4] I. Schuster,[5]

[1] Greg., *Ep.*, Lib. II, c. ii; P.L. LXXVII, 396: *Kyrieleison* autem nos neque diximus neque dicimus sicut a Graecis dicitur, quia in Graecis omnes simul dicunt, apud nos autem a clericis dicitur, a populo respondetur, et totidem uicibus etiam *Christe eleison* dicitur quod apud Graecos nullo modo dicitur. In cotidianis autem missis alia quae dici solent tacemus, tantummodo *Kyrieleison* et *Christe eleison* dicimus, ut in his deprecationis uocibus paulo diutius occupemur.

[2] *The English Rite*, London, 1915, II, p. 1021.

[3] *The Mass, A Study of the Roman Liturgy*, 2nd ed., London, 1937, p. 296.

[4] *Christian Worship*, Eng. trans., 5th ed., London, 1931, pp. 172–3.

[5] *The Sacramentary* (*Liber Sacramentorum*), E.T., London, 1925, II, pp. 21, 207.

P. Alfonzo,[1] A. Baumstark,[2] M. Cappuyns,[3] H. Leclercq.[4] The *Oremus* is certainly in the place where the *Orationes Sollemnes* were said, but none of the texts of the *Orationes Sollemnes* has the salutation *Dominus uobiscum*, nor indeed does *Oremus* come immediately before the Collect, but before the interval for silent prayer. In the bidding *Oremus* is always part of a sentence, as *Oremus, dilectissimi nobis, in primis pro ecclesia sancta dei*, etc. In view of this it does not seem likely, though it is possible, that the *Oremus* now standing at this point is a relic of a former introduction to the Solemn Prayers.

2. It may be that the surviving *Oremus* indicates the disappearance of the second collect which appears in a number of masses in the Leonine and Gelasian Sacramentaries. This view is held by A. Wilmart,[5] G. Dix,[6] B. Capelle,[7] A. G. Martimort,[8] A. Chavasse,[9] and F. Cabrol.[10] The first book of the Gelasian Sacramentary provides one, two, or three collects before the Secret, except for the Saturdays in Ember Weeks, which have six collects attached to the lessons. There are six examples of masses with three collects in the first book, St Stephen (I, vi, 30–2), St John Evangelist (I, vii, 36–8), the Innocents' Day (I, viii, 42–4), the Epiphany (I, xii, 61–3), the Wednesday after Pentecost (I, lxxxiii, 654–6), and the Octave of Pentecost (I, lxxxiii, 676–8).[11] All these masses have also an *Oratio ad populum*, which outside Lent is a sign of the antiquity of a mass.[12] These are, in fact, the most archaic formulae in the first book of the *Gelasianum*, implying, as they do, three lessons.[13] The third collect, though it does not bear this title, is the *Oratio super sindonem*.

The Good Friday rite in *Gelasianum* shows how the three collects were used.[14] The Priest says *Oremus*, and after the diaconal proclamations, *Flectamus genua* and *Leuate*, comes the first collect, *Deus a quo*

[1] *Oratio Fidelium*, Finalpia, 1928, pp. 62–6.

[2] *Missale Romanum*, Eindhoven, 1929, pp. 19–22.

[3] *Les Questions liturgiques et paroissiales*, 23, 1938, pp. 18–31.

[4] *D.A.C.L.*, art. "Messe", Vol. XI, col. 724.

[5] E. Bishop and A. Wilmart, *Le Génie du rit romain*, Paris, 1920, p. 87, n. 45.

[6] *The Shape of the Liturgy*, Westminster, 1945, pp. 491–2.

[7] "L'oeuvre liturgique de s. Gélase", in *J.T.S.*, N.S. 2, 1951, pp. 139–43; and *Trav. lit.*, II, 146–60.

[8] *L'Église en prière*, Paris, 1961, p. 360.

[9] *Le sacramentaire gélasien*, Tournai, 1958, p. 193; but see his article, "L'oraison 'super sindonem' dans la liturgie romaine", in *R.B.*, 70, Louvain, 1960, pp. 313–23.

[10] *D.A.C.L.*, IX, 1552.

[11] The numbering is from L. C. Mohlberg's edition.

[12] A. Chavasse, *Le sacramentaire gélasien*, p. 188.

[13] Ibid., p. 195.

[14] Ed. L. C. Mohlberg, I, xli, pp. 64 ff.

et Iudas, which is followed by the first lesson (from Hosea 6),[1] and a *responsorium*. Then comes the second collect, *Deus qui peccati ueteris*, followed by the second lesson (Exodus 12), and a *responsorium*, and then the Passion (according to St John), and then the Solemn Prayers, which doubtless originally occupied this place in all masses, but by the time of the original *Gelasianum* were confined to Good Friday, their place being filled by the third Collect, or *Oratio super sindonem*. The order of the lessons should be noted: it is not like the synagogue service, Law first and then Prophets, but an ascending order, first the Prophet (Hosea), then the Law (Exodus), as being the most important part of the Old Testament, and then the Gospel, as the most important of all.

So in masses with three prayers the first two were read before the first two lessons, the Prophecy and the Epistle, and the third collect after the Gospel. In masses with two collects before the Secret, the first is read before the Epistle, and the second after the Gospel. The one-collect type is the more primitive, being found in the ancient masses of the third, fourth and fifth Sundays in Lent, which were "scrutiny" masses.[2] The Ambrosian missal often adopts the second Gelasian collect (i.e. the one before the Secret) as its *Oratio super sindonem*, but these collects do not refer to the oblations, and were not Secrets, but were seasonal, and referred usually to the mystery of the day. The first Gelasian collect often refers to the mystery of the day, the second to the application of that mystery to the lives of the worshippers, and the third (or Secret) to the oblations. So the earliest tradition was that of one collect before the Secret, the later tradition that of two; and later still, at least from the time of Pope Gelasius, there were sometimes three. This second collect can hardly have existed side by side with the *Oratio fidelium* after the Gospel, and it seems reasonable to conclude that it replaced the *Oratio fidelium*, and did so at the time of Gelasius, who, as we have seen, transferred the main intercession to the beginning of the service in a Litany form. A hundred years later, St Gregory removed the second Gelasian collect.[3] It seems much more likely that the *Dominus uobiscum* and *Oremus* betray the omission of the second Gelasian collect than the omission of the Solemn Prayers.

[1] See e.g. the Lectionary of Alcuin, Nos. LXXXIIII, LXXXV, ed. A. Wilmart, *Ephemerides Liturgicae*, 1937, p. 155.

[2] M. Andrieu, *Les Ordines Romani*, II, 387.

[3] B. Capelle, *J.T.S.*, N.S. 2, pp. 139–43; *Trav. lit.*, II, 156–9; V. L. Kennedy, "The two collects of the Gelasian", in *Miscellanea Liturgica in honorem L. Cuniberti Mohlberg*, I, pp. 183–8, Rome, 1948.

3. J. A. Jungmann[1] thinks that the *Oremus* introduced the Secret. At the end of the fifth century the Secret would not in fact be secret, but be said aloud, like the Collect and the Post-Communion, and may therefore have been introduced by *Dominus uobiscum* and *Oremus*. The same view is held by H. A. P. Schmidt [2] and by E. Bourque.[3] If this is the case, the *Oremus* has been separated from the Secret by the subsequent addition of the offertory prayers.

The second theory seems the most likely of the three, as it fits in well with a change from the Solemn Prayers to the *Deprecatio Gelasii* at the end of the fifth century, accompanied by the insertion of the second collect of the *Gelasianum* either at the time of Gelasius or during the sixth century, and a further change at the time of St Gregory the Great, when the second collect disappeared, leaving the *Oremus* hanging in the air without a subsequent collect.

C. INTERCESSIONS IN THE NON-ROMAN WESTERN LITURGIES

Many of the non-Roman Western liturgies have general intercessions which perform the same kind of function as the Solemn Prayers of the Roman mass. That of the Stowe Missal stands apart from the others, both in its content and in its position in the mass. It alone is placed between the Epistle and the Gospel, after the Gradual, and it comes in a ferial mass. The others belong to the Vigil Service of Easter.

The Litany in the Stowe Missal is entitled *Deprecatio sancti martini pro populo*. The text is as follows:[4]

Deprecatio sancti martini pro populo incipit amen. deo gratias. Dicamus omnes domine exaudi et missere domine misserre:

Ex toto corde et ex tota menta. qui respices super terram et facis eam tremere: Oramus.

Pro altissima pace et trancillitate temporum nostrorum (IV) pro sancta aeclessia catholica quae est a finibus usque ad terminos orbis terrae (I): Oramus.

Pro pastore N. episcopo et omnibus episcopis et praespeteris et diaconis et omni clero (II, III): Oramus.

Pro hoc loco et inhabitantibus in eo pro pissimis imperatoribus et omni romano exercitu (IV): Oramus.

[1] *Missarum Sollemnia*, 2nd ed. Freiburg, 1958, I, p. 618.

[2] *Hebdomada Sancta*, ed. H. A. P. Schmidt, Rome, 1957, Vol. II, Sec. II, p. 784.

[3] *Études sur les sacramentaires romains*, Part I, *Les textes primitives*, Rome, 1948, p. 221.

[4] *The Stowe Missal*, ed. G. F. Warner, *H.B.S.*, XXXII, p. 6, London, 1915.

Pro omnibus qui in sublimitate constituti sunt pro uirginibus uiduis et orfanis (III, IV): Oramus.
Pro peregrinantibus et iter agentibus ac nauigantibus pro poenitentibus et catacominis (VI, V): Oramus.
Pro his qui in sancta ecclesia fructus misserecordiae largiuntur domine deus uirtutum exaudi preces nostras: Oramus.
etc.

The Roman numerals which have been added in brackets in this, as in the case of the other Litanies, refer to the *Orationes Sollemnes* by number when there is an agreement in subjects of intercession between these intercessions and those of the *Orationes Sollemnes.*

The other non-Roman prayers of intercession or litanies are connected with the Easter Vigil. Their position varies to some extent, and also their form, but they pray for the same, or similar, classes of people, and are generally twelve in number and begin with a prayer for the due keeping of Easter.

That in the Bobbio Missal, of the eighth century,[1] comes before the *Exultet*. It has no collects, but consists of biddings. Its subjects are as follows:

1. Thanksgiving for Easter. (No title.)
2. Pro his qui custodiarum uigiliis (*lege* uinculis) et captiuitate detenti pascha interesse non possunt (VI?).
3. Pro sacerdotibus ac ministris ecclesiae (III).
4. Pro uirgenibus (III).
5. Pro his qui elymosinas faciunt.
6. Pro peregrinantibus (VI).
7. Pro egrotis (VI).
8. Pro penetentibus.
9. Pro unitatem aeclesiae (I).
10. Pro pace populi et regum (IV).
11. Pro spiritibus pausancium.
12. Pro competentibus (V?).

Missale Gallicanum Vetus[2] has in Nos. 137 to 162 twelve biddings and twelve prayers, with a preliminary prayer for the whole Church. The titles of the twelve prayers are these:

[1] Ed. E. A. Lowe, *H.B.S.*, LVIII, pp. 67–9, Text; LXI, pp. 125–6, Notes: London, 1920 and 1923.
[2] Ed. L. C. Mohlberg, *Rerum Ecclesiasticarum Documenta*, Series Maior, Fontes, III, Rome, 1958, pp. 37–9.

1. Pro aeclesiae unitate (I).
2. Pro sacerdotibus et omne clero (III).
3. Pro regibus et pace (IV).
4. Pro uirginibus (III).
5. Pro uiduis et orfanis (III).
6. Pro egrotantibus (VI).
7. Pro captiuis uel qui in carceribus detenentur (VI).
8. Pro peregrinantibus (VI).
9. Pro elimosinis largitore.
10. Pro paenitentibus.
11. Pro neophitis (V?).
12. Pro conpetentibus (V?).

Missale Gothicum, a Gallican Sacramentary of the end of the seventh or beginning of the eighth century, has twelve biddings and prayers for use at the Easter Vigil:[1]

ORACIONES PASCHALIS DUODECIM CUM TOTIDEM COLLECTIONIBUS

1. Oracio pro Graciarum Accione. Prefacio. Oracio sequitur.
2. Oracio pro exsulibus.
3. Oracio pro sacerdotibus (III).
4. Oracio pro virginibus (III).
5. Oracio pro aelymosinas facientibus.
6. Oracio pro peregrinantibus (VI).
7. Oracio pro infirmis (VI).
8. Oracio pro paenitentibus.
9. Oracio pro unitate (I).
10. Oracio pro pace regum (IV).
11. Oracio pro spiritibus pausancium.
12. Oracio pro caticuminis (V).

In *Missale Gothicum* and *Missale Gallicanum Vetus* these prayers follow the Blessing of the Paschal Candle.

In the Mozarabic rite the structure is more like that of the Roman *Orationes Sollemnes*, in that the deacon proclaims the subject after the *Praefatio*, and the *Collectio* follows. This is the case in *Liber Ordinum*, though in the Mozarabic Missal the *praefatio* has disappeared. But in the Mozarabic books the intercessions do not follow one another continuously, as in the *Orationes Sollemnes* and in the Gallican litanies: they are divided by the lessons of the Paschal Vigil, and in *Liber Ordinum* the solemn Baptism is inserted after the third lesson. In *Liber*

[1] Ed. H. M. Banister, *H.B.S.*, Vol. LII, pp. 69–74, Text and Introduction, 1917; Vol. LIV, Notes and Indices, 1919.

Ordinum [1] each lesson is followed by a collect, a diaconal proclamation announcing the subject for intercession, and then another collect. Both collects in each case refer to the same subject of intercession, which is announced between them. *Post haec* (i.e. the Collect of the First Lesson) *clamat diaconus dicens,*

1. Pro solemnitate Pascali precemur Dominum.
2. Pro pace ecclesiarum et quiete populi precemur Dominum (IV?).
3. Pro sacerdotibus et ministris precemur Dominum (III).
4. Pro prosperitate principum et tranquillitate temporum precemur (IV).
5. Pro his qui huic sancte sollemnitati interesse non possunt, precemur Dominum.
6. Pro abundantia frugum et tranquillitate aerum precemur Dominum.
7. Pro uirginibus et continentibus precemur Dominum (III).
8. Pro his qui eleemosinas faciunt precemur Dominum.
9. Pro penitentibus et conpetentibus precemur Dominum (V?).
10. Pro perigrinantibus et nauigantibus precemur Dominum (VI).
11. Pro defunctorum requie et quiete precemur Dominum.

Missale Mozarabicum Mixtum [2] has the same general structure, and its ten intercessions are as follows:

1. Pro solemnitate paschali.
2. Pro his qui uariis necessitatibus detenti pasche interesse non possunt.
3. Pro sacerdotibus ac ministris (III).
4. Pro unitate fidei catholice (I).
5. Pro uirginibus (III).
6. Pro his qui elemosynas faciunt.
7. Pro peregrinantibus et nauigantibus. (VI)
8. Pro egrotis (VI).
9. Pro penitentibus.
10. Pro pace populi et regum (IV).

D. INTERCESSIONS IN THE ROMAN CANON

i. TE IGITUR

Since the disappearance before the end of the fifth century of any complete block of intercession (except on Good Friday), the Roman mass has contained no general intercession, but it has preserved to this

[1] Ed. Marius Férotin, *Monumenta Ecclesiae Liturgica*, Vol. V, *Le* Liber Ordinum *en usage dans l'Eglise Wisigothique et Mozarabe du cinquième au onzième siècle*, Paris, 1904, cols. 208 ff.

[2] P.L. 85, cols. 448 ff.

day petitions, forming part of the Canon, which are intercessory.[1] They are three in number, and are contained in *Te igitur* and in the Commemorations of the Living and the Departed.[2]

In *Te igitur* God is asked to accept and bless the gifts which are offered for the Holy Catholic Church.

> Te igitur clementissime pater per iesum christum filium tuum dominum nostrum supplices rogamus et petimus uti accepta habeas et benedicas haec dona haec munera haec sancta sacrificia inlibata in primis quae tibi offerimus pro ecclesia tua sancta catholica quam pacificare custodire adunare et regere digneris toto orbe terrarum una cum famulo tuo papa nostro illo.

This is the original pre-Gregorian text of this part of the Canon, going back to the fifth century and perhaps earlier. "Thy servant our pope" would at that time refer to the local bishop. The word *papa* is of Greek origin (πάππας, voc. πάπα) and occurs in classical authors, including Homer, where Nausicaa calls her father πάππα φιλ'.[3] It first appears in Latin in Juvenal,[4] and from about the beginning of the third century in Christian texts, where it is applied to bishops. St Cyprian is called *papa* by various correspondents.[5] This continued to be the usage in the fourth and fifth centuries: St Jerome, for instance, uses it to St Augustine,[6] as well as to Damasus, the Bishop of Rome.[7] Others call Augustine *papa*.[8] In the sixth century it comes to be more especially applied in the West to the Bishop of Rome, and in *Liber Pontificalis* replaces *episcopus* from Agapetus onwards (535–8). But this is not an exclusive rule till at least the seventh century.[9] As the Canon goes back to a much earlier time than that, it is likely that *papa nostro* simply means the bishop, that is to say the Pope in the Diocese of Rome, and the local bishop elsewhere.

Famulo tuo papa nostro illo is the reading of C and R, both ninth-century manuscripts of the Gregorian family. Here, as elsewhere, this family preserves an early form of the text, and the short text of this

[1] B. Capelle, "L'intercession dans la messe romaine" in *R.B.*, 65, Louvain, 1956, pp. 181–91; and *Travaux liturgiques*, II, 248–57.

[2] All texts from the Canon are cited from B. Botte, *Le Canon de la messe romaine, Édition critique*, Louvain, 1935; and the symbols of the manuscripts used in this section are in accordance with those used in Botte's edition, and listed by him on p. 29.

[3] *Od.*, VI, 57. [4] *Sat.*, VI, 652. [5] Cypr., *Epp.* 8, 23, 30, 31, 36.

[6] Hieron., *Epp.* 102, 103, 105, 112, 134, 141, 142, 143. [7] Hieron., *Ep.* 37.

[8] Aug., *Epp.* 199, 216.

[9] See P. de Labriolle, "Une exquisse de l'histoire du mot 'Papa'", in *Bulletin d'ancienne littérature et d'archéologie chrétiennes*, Vol. I, pp. 215–20, Paris, 1911.

passage goes back to a time before St Gregory the Great, when *papa* was applied to any bishop.

The next stage of development is the insertion before *famulo tuo* of the epithet *beatissimo*. This is to be found in S of the Irish family, RC[1] of the Gregorian, and A[2]GZX of the Gelasian. It is thus a widespread reading, and probably early: *beatissimus* is common in fourth-century inscriptions of Roman Emperors, and was also applied to ecclesiastical prelates.[1]

When in the sixth century the term *papa* begins to be restricted to the Bishop of Rome, some definition of the phrase *papa nostro illo* becomes desirable, and the words *sedis apostolicae* are added to show that it means the Pope and not the local bishop. This addition is found in the Bobbio Missal (B) and in the Stowe Missal (S), which adds a fuller phrase *episcopo sedis apostolicae*. Such an addition is also found in the second Solemn Prayer, in exactly the same forms as here in Bobbio and Stowe, and also in the early and later Gelasian authorities. *Sedis apostolicae* is a non-Roman kind of expression,[2] and so it is not surprising to find it in sources deriving from Gaul and Ireland. As it was not needed at Rome, it is not found in the *Hadrianum*, which is a papal sacramentary.

But if *papa* has come to mean the Pope, the local bishop, who hitherto had been mentioned under the title *papa*, has been extruded from the prayer, and so he is added again, in the form *et antistite nostro illo*. This occurs in more than one tradition, in the Gregorian (O), in the Gelasian (VAGZ), in the Milanese (MW), and in the Irish (B). Additions almost precisely similar to *sedis apostolicae* and *et antistite nostro* were made in the second of the Solemn Prayers in the same liturgical books.[3]

Finally, the petition is extended to cover the episcopate in general, for such is the meaning of the last phrase,

> et omnibus orthodoxis atque catholicae et apostolicae fidei cultoribus.

Words such as these are added by following authorities (variants within the phrase may be ignored for our purposes): OP[1] of the Gregorian, MW of the Milanese, BFS of the Irish, VΠG[1] of the Gelasian, family.

At first sight this phrase seems to refer to the faithful in general,[4]

[1] See Botte, *Le Canon de la messe romaine*, p. 54. [2] Ibid., p. 13.
[3] See pp. 42–3, below.
[4] *Cultor* often means simply "Christian", e.g. Prudentius, *Cath.*, VI, 125, *Cultor dei, memento.*

and it has been so taken by many commentators, but closer examination of it has led some to argue that it refers to the bishops in general, as the custodians of the true faith.[1] *Colere* can mean "to have care of", or "to be occupied with", and *cultor* can therefore bear the meaning of "custodian".

ii. COMMEMORATION OF THE LIVING

Te igitur is immediately followed by the *Memento* of the living, of which the Gregorian form is

> Memento domine famulorum famularumque tuarum et omnium circum adstantium quorum tibi fides cognita est et nota deuotio qui tibi offerunt hoc sacrificium laudis pro se suisque omnibus pro redemptione animarum suarum pro spe salutis et incolomitatis suae tibi reddunt uota sua aeterno deo uiuo et uero.

After *famularumque tuarum*, printed editions of the Missal from 1474 onwards add *N. et N.* to provide for the insertion of the names of persons to be specially commemorated. Many ancient texts of the Canon make such provision by rubric in this part of the prayer: for example, before *Memento* the Stowe Missal says

> Hic recitantur nomina uiuorum.

A corrector of the *Biblia Rossiana* lat. 204 (10th century), which belongs to the Gelasian family, says

> his nomina uiuorum memorentur non dominica die set tantum diebus priuatis.

and similarly Pseudo-Amalarius prescribes

> hoc nomina uiuorum memorentur si uolueris sed non dominica die nisi caeteris diebus.

This is parallel to the situation with regard to the *Memento* of the Departed, which until the ninth century was not said at Sunday masses, but only on weekdays. Nevertheless it is probable that the commemoration of the living was originally made at all masses. In the Gelasian tradition *Vaticanus Reginensis* 316 and the Sacramentary of Angoulême

[1] B. Capelle, "L'intercession dans la messe romaine", in *R.B.*, 65, Louvain, 1956, p. 187; *Trav. lit.*, II, 254; "Et omnibus orthodoxis atque apostolicae fidei cultoribus", in *Miscellanea historica in honorem Alberti de Meyer*, I, pp. 137–50, Louvain, 1946; *Trav. lit.*, II, 258–68; B. Botte et C. Mohrmann, *L'Ordinaire de la messe*, *Études liturgiques*, 2, Paris-Louvain, 1953, p. 76, note (c), p. 77, note 2.

provide for a special mention of the king, adding at the beginning

> memento domine famulo tuo rege nostro illo (A)

or

> memento deus rege nostro cum omni populo (V);

this appears to be an addition made in the Frankish kingdom and not at Rome.

After *deuotio* certain authorities add, as does the modern text of the Missal, *pro quibus tibi offerimus uel*. The texts which support this addition are OP²A²M, all of the ninth century, and the Missal of 1474.

The *Memento* of the living is evidently the diptychs of the living, commemorating in particular the worshippers present who are the offerers. It is clear from the letter of Innocent I to Decentius, Bishop of Gubbio, written in 416, that at that date it stood in its present position, immediately following *Te igitur* and closely connected with it; and that it was very likely expressed in terms similar to those of the present form.[1] Innocent says:

> De nominibus uero recitandis antequam precem sacerdos faciat atque eorum oblationes quorum nomina recitanda sunt sua oratione commendat, quam superfluum sit, et ipse pro tua prudentia recognoscis, ut cuius hostiam necdum Deo offeras, eius ante nomen insinues quamuis illi incognitum sit nihil. Prius ergo oblationes sunt commendandae, ac tunc eorum nomina quorum sunt edicenda, ut inter sacra mysteria nominentur, non inter alia quae ante praemittimus, ut ipsis mysteriis uiam futuris precibus aperiamus.[2]

The recital of the names, according to Innocent, should not be made before the priest *precem faciat*, and *prex* is the Canon, the great Eucharistic Prayer. That is to say, it does not come before the Offertory, but is placed *inter sacra mysteria*, since it must follow the *commendatio oblationum*, and not precede it. There is nothing in the Canon before the *Memento* of the living except the Preface and *Te igitur*, and the latter does in fact constitute the commendation or offering of the gifts:

> rogamus et petimus uti accepta habeas et benedicas haec dona haec munera haec sancta sacrificia inlibata quae tibi offerimus.

[1] B. Capelle, "Innocent Ier. et le canon de la messe", in *Recherches de théologie ancienne et mediévale*, 19, Louvain, 1952, pp. 5–16; and *Trav. lit.*, II, 248–57.

[2] Innocent I, *Ep.*, XXV (P.L. 20, 553). The passage is discussed by R. H. Connolly in *J.T.S.*, XX, London, 1919, pp. 215–26; F. E. Brightman, in *J.T.S.*, XXIII, London, 1922, p. 410; J. H. Srawley, *Early History of the Liturgy*, Cambridge, 1947, p. 173; and by B. Capelle, art. cit.

It is followed, as Innocent says that it ought to be, by the *Memento*, which is the prayer for the offerers.

iii. COMMEMORATION OF THE DEPARTED

The earliest form of this Commemoration is

> Memento etiam domine famulorum famularumque tuarum ill. et ill. qui nos praecesserunt cum signo fidei et dormiunt in somno pacis ipsis et omnibus in christo quiescentibus locum refrigerii lucis et pacis ut indulgeas deprecamur per christum dominum nostrum.

Many of the ancient witnesses of the Roman Canon omit this section altogether, and pass straight from *Supplices te rogamus* to *Nobis quoque peccatoribus*. Among them the most ancient are the Gregorian *Hadrianum* (CR) and the Gelasian VAGII. The Sacramentary of Angoulême adds, however, in its place, a commemoration of the departed in quite different words. The *Memento* is present in this place in O and Padua D.47 of the Gregorian family, in the whole of the Irish family, and in *Ordo Romanus* VII. The explanation of these facts is that until the ninth century it was not a part of the Canon at every mass: it was used only in masses of the dead, and in weekday masses, but was not said on Sundays or feasts.[1] *Ordo* VII has

> memento etiam domine et eorum nominum qui nos praecesserunt cum signo fidei et dormiunt in somno pacis. *Et recitantur. Deinde postquam recitata fuerint, dicit:* Ipsis domine et omnibus in Christo quiescentibus locum refrigerii lucis et pacis ut indulgeas deprecamur. Per Christum dominum nostrum.[2]

and before *memento* it has a rubric

> *Hic orationes duae dicuntur una super dypticios altera post lectionem nominum, et hoc cottidianis uel in agendis tantummodo diebus.*

The *Canones S. Gregorii* in the Penitential of St Theodore of Canterbury say

> Secundum Romanos die dominico nomina mortuorum non recitantur ad missam.[3]

[1] M. Andrieu, *Les Ordines Romani du haut moyen âge*, II, pp. 273 ff., Louvain, 1948; Edmund Bishop, *Liturgica Historica*, Oxford, 1918, pp. 96 ff., 109 ff.; B. Botte, *Le Canon de la messe romaine*, Louvain, 1935, pp. 67–9; A. G. Martimort, *L'église en prière*, Paris, 1961, pp. 408–9.

[2] M. Andrieu, *Les Ordines Romani*, II, p. 301.

[3] Ibid., II, p. 276.

And even as late as the eleventh century a sacramentary of Florence inserts in the Canon before this *Memento* a rubric

Hec non dicit in dominicis diebus nec in aliis festiuitatibus maioribus.[1]

This commemoration is not contained in the canon of the *Hadrianum*, which was a papal book, providing for Sunday and stational masses, and not for weekday masses at which the *Memento* of the dead would be used at Rome. But it does occur in *Hadrianum* in a mass *super episcopum defunctum*. It is absent from the old Gelasian book, and for the same reason, that the Canon in *Gelasianum*, which is in the third book, follows a series of sixteen ferial masses with which that book opens, and which are entitled

Orationes et preces cum canone per dominicis diebus.

On the other hand, books which provide the Canon in weekday masses include the *Memento* of the Departed. This is the case with the Bobbio Missal, which includes it in a *Missa romensis cotidiana*, and with Padua D.47, where it is in a mass which is the seventh of a group headed

Incipiunt orationes cottidianae Gregorii papae.

So also in *Missale Francorum*, where it is under the heading

Incipiunt preces communes cottidianae cum canone.

To omit this commemoration on Sundays was Roman use, but the Gallican practice was to include it at all times.[2] From the ninth century onwards it was more and more frequently included in the Canon, and eventually became a fixed part of the Canon. Its present form of words

famulorum famularumque tuarum

which is parallel to the form of the *Memento* of the living, is probably due to Alcuin, and the earlier form is

et eorum nomina.

It may well be that the extension of its use to Sundays began by allowing departed persons of great eminence, such as sovereigns and bishops, to be thus commemorated on Sundays. *Ordo* XV, of the second half of the eighth century, says

[1] Andrieu, *Les Ordines Romani*, II, 276. [2] Ibid., p. 278, n. 4.

In diebus autem septimane, de secunda feria quod est usque in die sabbato, celebrantur missas uel nomina eorum (=mortuorum) commemorant.

Die autem dominica non celebrantur agendas mortuorum nec nomina eorum ad missas recitantur, sed tantum uiuorum nomina regum uel principum seu et sacerdotum, uel pro omni populo christiano oblationis uel uota redduntur.[1]

Padua D.47 has a rubric before the *Memento* in the following terms,

si fuerint nomina defunctorum recitentur dicente diacono ("Memento etiam domine . . .").

Professor Ratcliff accordingly suggests that originally the deacon said this prayer aloud, while the celebrant proceeded with the silent recitation of the Canon, and that it became a fixed part of the Canon at the time when the priest, celebrating low mass without a deacon, took over the parts of the liturgy which had formerly belonged to the deacon.[2]

Though this prayer only came into constant use at a later period, it is clear from its language that it is both Roman and ancient.[3] *Praecesserunt*, *signo fidei* (= baptism), *in somno pacis* and *refrigerium* have all an archaic ring. Furthermore, the *quoque* in the next section *Nobis quoque peccatoribus* fits well after the Commemoration of the Departed,

ipsis et omnibus in christo quiescentibus locum refrigerii lucis et pacis ut indulgeas deprecamur . . . nobis quoque peccatoribus famulis tuis . . . partem aliquam et societatem donare digneris cum. . . .

But it does not fit at all well after the conclusion of *Supplices te rogamus*, which is

. . . omni benedictione caelesti et gratia repleamur per christum dominum nostrum. Nobis quoque peccatoribus . . .

[1] *Ordo* XV, 128–30, in M. Andrieu, op. cit., III, pp. 121–2.
[2] E. C. Ratcliff, "Christian Worship and Liturgy", in *The Study of Theology*, ed. K. E. Kirk, London, 1939, p. 441.
[3] Edmund Bishop, *Liturgica Historica*, p. 98; B. Botte, *Le Canon de la messe romaine*, pp. 68–9.

3. *The Content and Form of the Solemn Prayers*

A. CONTENT

The *Orationes Sollemnes* were certainly in existence in the Roman rite before the end of the fifth century, for it was at that time, between 492 and 496, that they were removed from the Ordinary of the Mass by Gelasius, who substituted his new Litany at the beginning of the mass. It seems fairly certain that the Solemn Prayers were there before the middle of the fifth century. St Prosper of Aquitania testifies to the existence of intercessions in the mass in words which have close similarity to the text of the *Orationes Sollemnes*. The document called *Praeteritorum sedis apostolicae episcoporum auctoritates de gratia Dei*, which is annexed to the letter of Pope Celestinus I to the Bishops of Gaul, which was written about 431, is from the hand of Prosper, and was probably written at Rome about 435–42.[1] The treatise *De Vocatione gentium* was also written, about 450, by Prosper.[2]

The similarities between the Solemn Prayers and the references in these two treatises of Prosper are brought out by Dom R. H. Connolly [3] and by Dom M. Cappuyns.[4] The *Auctoritates* cite the intercessions of the Church in the following terms:

> . . . obsecrationum quoque sacerdotalium sacramenta respiciamus, quae ab apostolis tradita in toto mundo atque in omni ecclesia catholica uniformiter celebrantur; ut legem credendi lex statuat supplicandi. Cum enim sanctarum plebium praesules mandata sibimet legatione fungantur, apud diuinam clementiam humani generis agunt causam, et tota secum ecclesia congemiscente postulant et precantur,
>
> 1. ut infidelibus donetur fides,
> 2. ut *idololatrae* ab impietatis suae *liberentur* erroribus,

[1] M. Cappuyns, "L'origine des Capitula pseudo-célestiens contre le semi-pélagianisme", in *R.B.*, 41, Maredsous, 1929, pp. 156–70.

[2] M. Cappuyns, "L'auteur du De Vocatione Omnium Gentium", in *R.B.*, 39, Maredsous, 1927, pp. 198–226.

[3] "Liturgical Prayers of Intercession, I: The Good Friday Orationes Sollemnes", in *J.T.S.*, XXI, pp. 219 ff., Oxford, 1920.

[4] M. Cappuyns, "Les Orationes Sollemnes du vendredi saint", in *Les Questions liturgiques et paroissiales*, 23, Louvain, 1938, pp. 18–31.

3. ut *Iudaeis ablato cordis uelamine* lux ueritatis appareat,
4. ut *haeretici* catholicae fidei perceptione *resipiscant,*
5. ut schismatici spiritum rediuiuae caritatis accipiant,
6. ut lapsis poenitentiae remedia conferantur,
7. ut denique catechumenis ad *regenerationis sacramenta* perductis caelestis *misericordiae aula reseretur.*[1]

No. 1 is parallel in subject to the ninth Solemn Prayer, for pagans, and the diaconal proclamation asks that they may forsake their idols and be turned to the true God, which is the equivalent of asking that faith may be granted to them. But there is no verbal similarity here between Prosper and the Solemn Prayers.

No. 2 is also parallel to the ninth Solemn Prayer, and *idololatrae . . . liberentur* may be compared with "et *libera* eos *ab idolorum cultura*".

No. 3 is parallel to the eighth Solemn Prayer, for the Jews, and *ablato cordis uelamine* is similar to "ut deus et dominus noster *auferat uelamen de cordibus eorum*".

No. 4 is related to No. VII of the Solemn Prayers, for heretics and schismatics. *Hereticis* in the bidding, and "*heretica* peruersitate" in the collect may be compared with *haeretici* in Prosper, and the verb *resipiscant* is common to both.

No. 5 is also related to No. VII of the Solemn Prayers, and both mention schismatics, but there is no other verbal similarity.

No. 7 is related to the fifth Solemn Prayer, for catechumens. *Catechumenis* is common to both; *adaperiat . . . ianuamque misericordiae* is related to *misericordiae aula reseretur* in thought, and *lauacrum regenerationis* to *regenerationis sacramenta.*

No. 6 of Prosper, the prayer for the lapsed, has no parallel in the text of the Solemn Prayers as they are known from the eighth century onwards. But it is quite possible, perhaps likely, that in Prosper's day in the fifth century they did still contain such a prayer. The Roman clergy, writing to St Cyprian, and speaking of the general intercessions of the Church, and quite possibly having in mind some early form of the *Oratio fidelium* at mass, requests prayers for the lapsed and the *stantes.*[2] St Leo the Great mentions the lapsed after the catechumens.[3]

The *De Vocatione* of Prosper furnishes further parallels to the Solemn Prayers.

[1] R. H. Connolly, "Liturgical Prayers of Intercession; I. The Good Friday Orationes Sollemnes", in *J.T.S.*, XXI, pp. 219–20.

[2] Cypr., *Ep.*, XXXI, vi; P.L. IV, 321: Oremus pro lapsis ut erigantur, oremus pro stantibus ut non ad ruinas usque tententur . . .

[3] Leo, *Serm.*, xlix (De Quad. xi), 3; P.L. LIV, 303.

... Quam legem supplicationis (*sc.* 1 Tim. 2. 1, 2) ita omnium sacerdotum et omnium fidelium deuotio concorditer tenet, ut nulla pars mundi sit in qua huiusmodi orationes non celebrentur a populis christianis. Supplicat ergo ubique ecclesia Deo non solum pro sanctis et in Christo regeneratis, sed etiam *pro omnibus infidelibus* et inimicis crucis Christi, et *pro omnibus idolorum cultoribus,* pro omnibus qui Christum in membris ipsius persequuntur, *pro Iudaeis,* quorum caecitati lumen euangelii non refulget, *pro haereticis et schismaticis,* qui ab unitate fidei et caritatis alieni sunt. Quid autem pro istis petit nisi *ut relictis erroribus suis conuertantur ad Deum,* accipiant fidem, accipiant caritatem, et de ignorantiae tenebris liberati in agnitionem ueniant ueritatis.[1]

With *pro omnibus idolorum cultoribus* compare *ab idolorum cultura* in Solemn Prayer IX; *pro Iudaeis* with Solemn Prayer VIII, noting also *caecitati* in Prosper, and *obcaecatione* in Solemn Prayer IX; with *pro haereticis et schismaticis* compare Solemn Prayer VII; and with *relictis erroribus suis conuertantur ad Deum* compare the ninth Solemn Prayer, *et relictis idolis suis conuertantur ad Deum.*

These agreements of Prosper are with the collects as well as with the biddings, so it is clear that in his day the biddings and collects must have been united. We shall see later that their style and content shows them to be from different hands, but by the fifth century they must have been united as they have been since. Prosper says that the practice of general intercession is apostolic,[2] and this is true, for it depends upon 1 Timothy 2. 1. He says that the prayers are used daily, at least the prayer for the enemies of the Church is so used, and if so, no doubt the rest of the *Oratio Fidelium.*[3]

It is uncertain how far the Solemn Prayers can be traced back in their present form. The orders of bishop, priest, deacon, subdeacon, acolyte, exorcist, reader and doorkeeper are enumerated in the same order as in the letter of Pope Cornelius to Fabius of Antioch in 251.[4] The occurrence of confessors in the ecclesiastical orders enumerated in the bidding of the third prayer seems to point to an age of persecution, that is to say, not later than 311, the end of the persecution of Diocletian. By the fifth century there were no persecutions and therefore no confessors in the strict sense. But does the term bear the original meaning

[1] Prosper, *De Voc.*, i, 12; P.L. LI, 664.

[2] *Responsiones ad capitula obiectionum Vincentianarum*, 2. P.L. LI, 179 B: Apostolus ... sollicitissime praecipit, quod in omnibus ecclesiis piissime custoditur, ut Deo pro omnibus hominibus supplicetur; *Auctoritates*, quoted on pp. 39–40 above.

[3] *Contra Collatorem*, 12; P.L. LI, 245 B: Ecclesia quotidie pro inimicis suis orat, id est pro his qui nondum Deo crediderunt.

[4] Eusebius, *Hist. Eccles.*, VI, 43, 11, ed. G. Bardy, II, 156. Paris, 1953.

of confessor in this bidding? In St Cyprian a confessor is a man persecuted for his faith, but not suffering death and becoming thereby a martyr.[1] It has been thought that in the Solemn Prayers it carries a different and later meaning; that it signifies *continentes* or else *cantores* (singers), who "confess" God by praising him, according to a common Christian use of *confiteor*. This view is supported by the fact that in the bidding of Solemn Prayer III confessors come between doorkeepers and virgins, which might be a natural position for singers.[2] On the other hand, confessors are associated with widows and virgins (as here) as early as the *Apostolic Tradition* of Hippolytus.[3] They were an ecclesiastical order, and enjoyed certain clerical privileges.[4] On the whole it seems likely that confessors in the Solemn Prayers go back to the age of persecution, to the early fourth, and perhaps to the third, century, to the time of St Cyprian, as Baumstark and Jungmann thought.[5] The language of No. VI, *aperiat carceres, uincula dissoluat*, also seems more applicable to Christians imprisoned for the faith than to ordinary criminals or prisoners of war.

The second Solemn Prayer, for "our pope", shows a development precisely similar to that which has already been discussed in connection with the text of *Te igitur* in the Canon.[6] In the Solemn Prayers *beatissimo* is read by all three families, the Gallican, the Gregorian, and RS of the Gelasian of the eighth century, as it is by the Gelasian and Gregorian families in the Canon. As we saw in discussing the Canon, this feature points to the fourth century. The original form of the bidding, as of *Te igitur*, read simply *papa nostro*, meaning the local bishop. The Gelasian manuscripts add *sedis apostolicae* to define the meaning of *papa*, and to show that it now means the Pope and not the local bishop, and such a development will not be earlier than the sixth century. They further add *et pro antistite nostro*. Neither of these additions is to be found in the Old Gallican or the Gregorian, which here represent

[1] H. Delehaye, "Martyr et confesseur", in *Analecta Bollandiana*, 39, pp. 20–49, Brussels, 1921, especially p. 31.

[2] H. Delehaye, op. cit.; G. Morin, "Notes d'ancienne littérature chrétienne, 1. Que faut-il entendre par les confessores auxquels était addressé le traité de Macrobe le donatiste?" in *R.B.*, 29, pp. 82–4, Maredsous, 1912.

[3] *Didascaliae apostolorum fragmenta ueronensia latina*, XXXIV, ed. E. Hauler, Leipzig, 1900, pp. 48–9.

[4] Hippolytus, *Apostolic Tradition*, X, ed. G. Dix, p. 18.

[5] Albert Michael Koeniger, *Beitrage zur Geschichte des christlichen Altertums . . . Festgabe Albert Ehrhard*, Bonn–Leipzig, 1922, art. "Liturgischer Nachhall aus der Verfolgungszeit", by A. Baumstark, pp. 53–72, esp. p. 60; J. A. Jungmann, *Missarum Sollemnia*, 2nd ed., Freiburg, 1958, Vol. I, p. 618.

[6] Above, pp. 32–3.

an earlier situation, going back before the sixth century. The Gelasians have made the consequential alteration from singular to plural in the Collect attached to this bidding.

It is more difficult to trace the development of the fourth Bidding and Prayer, for the civil authority. The St Gall manuscript of the Gelasian prays for "our most Christian emperors", the Gregorian for "our most Christian emperor", in the singular; the Gallican for "most Christian kings"; and the other three Gelasians embrace both emperors and kings: "our most Christian emperors or our king N." (R); "our most Christian emperor or our king N." (V); "our most Christian emperor or king N." (A). Similarly the Collect asks God to look upon the Roman Empire (or the Empire of the Romans) in all the traditions, except *Ottobonianus*, which speaks of the Christian empire; and to this the Gelasian adds a mention of the Franks.[1]

"King" is not a Roman term, and therefore not likely to be used at any time of the Roman Emperors. It is a Frankish term, and is an addition, outside Rome, made at any time after about 475. It is safe therefore to conclude that any reading which speaks of king or kings is a later modification, and that the original will be a text referring only to the Roman Emperor or Emperors. This is to be found in the St Gall manuscript of the Gelasian (plural) and in the Gregorian (singular), and these are earlier in date than the readings of the remaining Gelasians or the Gallican. "Most Christian" would be inappropriate before Constantine, and also after 337, since Constantius and Constans were inclined to Arianism, or under Julian, a pagan. Julian's successor Jovian, a decided Christian, might be so described, but he reigned for a very short time. Gratian and Theodosius, and Arcadius and Honorius, covering the period from 375 to 408, would very well fit such a term as *christianissimis imperatoribus nostris*. Andrieu suggests that the text of S, *christianissimis imperatoribus nostris*, reflects the situation between September 813, when Louis the Debonair was associated with Charlemagne, and 28 January 814, when Charlemagne died.[2] This might well be the date of the manuscript, Sangallensis 348. But is the text contemporary with this manuscript? The text of the Solemn Prayers in this manuscript is one of the most ancient available, and this phrase might in fact be centuries older than the date of the manuscript; and the biddings, in one of which this phrase occurs, are in general older

[1] See the text and apparatus, above, p. 15.

[2] M. Andrieu, "A propos de quelques sacramentaires récemment édités", in *Revue des sciences religieuses*, 2, Paris, 1922, p. 205.

than the text of the collects, and may go back to the fourth century. Indeed, this same manuscript in the prayer *pro beatissimo papa nostro* has a form which is certainly much earlier than the ninth century, and must be before the sixth, since the *papa* is here the bishop and not the Pope of Rome.

Nevertheless, the text of this prayer may well have been altered, and perhaps more than once, in the period between the fourth century, when it seems likely, on linguistic and other grounds, that the biddings were drawn up, and the eighth century, when we see the text in the earliest surviving manuscripts. It is therefore impossible to be sure what the original form was. The reference to a Christian Emperor or Emperors is found in all the manuscripts considered except in the Old Gallican, which has dropped the Roman Emperor, and prays *pro christianissimis regibus*, who sound like the kings of the Frankish kingdoms. But curiously enough, though S has this phrase in the bidding, it allows *Romanum . . . imperium* to stand in the text of the collect, and it does not even add *atque Francorum*, as the Gelasian tradition usually does; and it is a Roman book (Gregorian C) which substitutes *christianum* for *romanum* in this phrase. It is in Gaul that we should expect to find such a substitution. *Romanum, romanorum* are Roman expressions, within the Empire, and *christianum* replaces *romanum* in Gaul, as may be seen from Merovingian and Carolingian liturgical books, which make such changes, whereas the earliest manuscript of the *Gelasianum* repeatedly uses *Romanum* in its masses for war-time.[1]

The *Deprecatio Gelasii* invites prayers

> pro religiosis principibus omnique militia eorum (*Paris*, 1153)

or

> pro domno illo imperatore nostro, iudicibus et exercitibus eius (*Angelica*, B.3.18).

Neither form refers to the Emperor as *christianissimus*, and the second is non-committal, and simply prays for the emperor without any indication of his spiritual status. The first is less vague, but avoids the term *christianissimus* and could have served well in the time of

[1] *Gel.* III, lvi–lxi (ed. L. C. Mohlberg, pp. 213–17); see A. Chavasse, *Le sacramentaire gélasien*, p. 436; G. Tellenbach, *Römischer und christlicher Reichsgedanke in der Liturgie des frühen M.A.*, in *Sitzungsberichte* (Acad. de Heidelberg, Phil.-Hist. Kl.), 1934, pp. 4–54; L. Biehl, *Das liturgische Gebet für Kaiser und Reich*, Paderborn, 1937.

St Gelasius, between 493 and 496, for use of the King of the Goths, Theodoric, an Arian who on the whole was tolerant of the Church, and gave liberty of worship to Catholics and did not interfere in episcopal elections unless disorder arose.

We shall probably therefore be safe in believing that the Roman mass had a general intercession after the Gospel from the times of St Justin Martyr, and probably indeed from the first century, by which it put into practice the apostolic injunction of 1 Timothy 2. 1; and that it had the Solemn Prayers in something like the present form from, say, the middle of the fourth century, and the Biddings possibly from a slightly earlier date.[1]

B. FORM

The form in which the Solemn Prayers are cast is ancient. The officiant stands before the altar, and desires the prayers of the people for a particular object:

Oremus, dilectissimi nobis, in primis pro . . . (I).
Oremus et pro . . . (II–V, VII–IX).
Oremus, dilectissimi nobis, deum patrem omnipotentem ut . . . (VI).

At the end of the bidding he reiterates the summons to prayer, *Oremus*; and then the deacon proclaims *Flectamus genua*, and all kneel for silent prayer. After an interval the deacon calls, *Leuate*, and the officiant then says the collect. The deacon's command to bow the knee, and then to stand up, is paralleled in the κλίνωμεν γόνυ and ἀναστῶμεν of the Coptic formulary for Lent, and the series of invitations to prayer, and prayers said by the deacon in the baptismal rite of the Ethiopians, may also be compared with it.[2]

We have seen [3] that by the middle of the fifth century, in the time of Prosper of Aquitania, the biddings and the collects of the Solemn Prayers were already united. But it is clear that they do not proceed from the same hand, and were not composed together as one set. The literary style of the biddings and the collects is quite different. The biddings are as long as, and in some cases longer than, the collects; and

[1] See also M. Cappuyns, "Les Orationes Sollemnes du vendredi saint", in *Les Questions liturgiques et paroissiales*, 23, Louvain, 1938, pp. 18–31; P. Alfonzo, *Oratio Fidelium*, Finalpia, 1928, p. 65; A. Baumstark, *Missale Romanum*, Eindhoven, 1929, pp. 20–1.

[2] P.L. 138, 938–43. See also A. Baumstark, *Comparative Liturgy*, London, 1958, pp. 77–8.

[3] See p. 41, above.

in nearly all cases they are more detailed. They both list the persons and classes of persons to be prayed for, and, except in the case of No. III, they specify the purpose of the petition. The collects tend to be more general in their petitions, and to have the restraint which is characteristic of the Latin collect of the best period. They are in the concise and disciplined style of good Roman liturgical prose, and have nothing of the florid and rhetorical atmosphere of a Gallican Latin formulary. Moreover, the collects are carefully composed according to the rhythmic rules of Latin *cursus*. As this style of composition prevailed from the fourth to the seventh century, it is useless as a criterion for dating a document composed within this period, though it does suggest that the collects of the Solemn Prayers are not likely to go back to a period before the fourth century. But the biddings very rarely conform to the rules of *cursus*, and may well date from before the fourth century. In the fourth and fifth centuries the earlier quantitative prosody in Latin gave way by a gradual process to one based on accentuation. The *cursus* of the Solemn Prayers is throughout based on accentuation and not on quantity, and so it may be said with confidence that the collects are not earlier than the fourth century, though the biddings may be, and in any case the two sets are not by the same hand.[1]

We take the biddings first, and discover that observance of the *cursus* is very rare. It does not occur at all in the biddings of Nos. I, II, III, IV, V, VIII, or IX. In No. VI we have

púrget erróribus	(*tardus*)
salútis indúlgeat	(*tardus*)

in No. VII

erróribus uniuérsis	(*uelox*)
reuocáre dignétur	(*planus*)

In the Collects rhythmic endings abound, and none of the nine is without at least one of them.

I.	géntibus reuelásti	(*uelox*)
II.	uniuérsa fundántur	(*planus*)
	pietáte consérua	(*planus*)
	méritis augeátur	(*uelox*)

[1] On the *cursus* in liturgical prose see E. Vacandard, "Le cursus: son origine, son histoire, son emploi dans la liturgie", in *Revue des questions historiques*, 78, Paris, 1905, pp. 59–102; *Dict. d'arch. chrét. et de lit.*, III, 2, cols. 3193 ff., art. "Cursus", by H. Leclercq; on the *cursus* in general A. C. Clark, *The cursus in Medieval and Vulgar Latin*, Oxford, 1910; *Fontes Prosae Numerosae*, Oxford, 1909; L. Laurand, *Ce qu'on sait et ce qu'on ignore du Cursus*, Louvain-Paris, 1914; M. G. Nicolau, *L'origine du Cursus rythmique et les débuts de l'accent d'intensité en latin*, Paris, 1930.

III.	ordínibus supplicántes	(*uelox*)
	fidéliter seruiátur	(*uelox*)
IV.	potestáte domináris	(*trispondaic*)
	benígnus impérium	(*tardus*)
	poténtia comprimántur	(*uelox*)
V.	próle fecúndas	(*planus*)
	fíliis aggregéntur	(*uelox*)
VI.	laborántium fortitúdo	(*uelox*)
	tribulatióne clamántium	(*tardus*)
	gaúdeant adfuísse	(*uelox*)
VII.	fraúde decéptas	(*planus*)
	córda resipíscant	(*trispondaic*)
	rédeant firmítátem	(*uelox*)
VIII.	obcaecatióne deférimus	(*tardus*)
	tenébris eruántur	(*trispondaic*)
IX.	sémper inquíris	(*planus*)

The very striking difference in rhythmic structure between the language of the collects and that of the biddings establishes beyond doubt that they were composed separately, and only subsequently united in this form of intercession. Comparison of the collects and biddings also shows that in no case does the collect repeat any phrase of the bidding: it prays for the same persons, and often reproduces the same ideas, but never in the same words. (The only exception to this is "pro perfidis iudaeis" in the bidding, and "iudaicam perfidiam" in the collect, of No. VIII.) Taken together with the difference in rhythm, this clearly demonstrates that the biddings and the collects were composed by different persons, and very likely at different times.

Conclusion

The Good Friday rite of *Missale Romanum* at the present day shows many signs of its great antiquity. It preserves three lessons, of which two are from the Old Testament, and in the striking order of Prophecy and Law; it preserves the intercession of the faithful in the form of the *Orationes Sollennes*, at the old position, beginning the Mass of the Faithful; and it preserves the ancient Communion from the reserved sacrament which was once used on aliturgical days which had no offering of the sacrifice. It seems clear that the Solemn Prayers as they stand now in the Missal, and as they stood there in the eighth century, at which time we have the earliest surviving manuscripts of the Sacramentaries, must go back a good deal further than the eighth century. They were removed from daily use by Gelasius, when he substituted his *Deprecatio* at the beginning of mass. It is not possible to be certain how far the Solemn Prayers go back before that time. From what Prosper of Aquitania has to say, we can conclude that they were in use in something like the present form in the middle of the fifth century. They may well have been used in something very like this form in the fourth century. Apart from the prayer for the Emperor, which has been altered in any case, they could go back to the days of persecution, and indeed it seems very likely, from what St Justin and later writers say, that some prayers of intercession were offered at this point in the mass from the second century onwards, and possibly from the first. It seems reasonable, from the internal evidence of the prayers, and the study of their rhythm, to conclude that the Collects go back to the fourth century, and the biddings earlier, perhaps the early fourth century, and perhaps even the third.

Gelasius (492–6) replaced these prayers by his Litany or *Deprecatio*, which covered similar ground, but was constructed in a very different form, and it was placed at the beginning of the mass, so that the prayers now came before the scripture readings, as in the old synagogue service. This *Deprecatio* did not survive for more than a century, for at the end of the sixth century, in the time of St Gregory the Great, or before, it had been reduced to the *Kyrie eleison*, which has ever since retained its place at the beginning of the Roman mass. The Roman rite was thus left with nothing by way of intercession except the Solemn Prayers in full on Good Friday, and for daily use the brief intercessions which form part of the Canon.

II

Ember Days

1. *Origins*

The observance of the seasonal fasts later called *Quattuor Tempora* was for a long time peculiar to Roman Liturgy, that is to the rite of the City of Rome. It only spread gradually, with the diffusion of the Roman rite, to the whole of the Western Church, first to Naples and to England in the seventh century, then to Gaul in the eighth, to Spain as late as the eleventh, and to Milan in the twelfth.[1] Since then it has continued as a fixed feature of the Roman Missal. The first Roman authority to speak of the Embertides is St Leo the Great (440–61), who preached many sermons on these occasions,[2] but in his time they were already an ancient institution. How far back can they be traced?

Their origin was unknown to St Leo, and to all subsequent writers: evidently they were so ancient that their precise origin had been forgotten. *Liber Pontificalis* attributes to St Callistus (217–22) the institution of the Saturday fast at these seasons:

> hic constituit ieiunium die sabbati ter in anno fieri frumenti uini et olei secundum prophetiam.[3]

The reference to the prophecy is to Zech. 8. 19:

> Haec dicit Dominus exercituum: Ieiunium quarti et ieiunium quinti et ieiunium septimi et ieiunium decimi erit domui Iuda in gaudium et laetitiam et in solemnitates praeclaras.

The weekly stational fasts of Wednesday and Friday are of great antiquity, and older than St Callistus, and *Liber Pontificalis* may be right in attributing to this Pope the addition of a fast on Saturday in the Ember Weeks. The notice in *Liber Pontificalis* mentions only three seasons in the year, the times of the harvests of corn, wine, and oil, which correspond to the Ember Fasts of the fourth, seventh, and tenth months, June, September, and December.

[1] A. G. Martimort, *L'église en prière, Introduction à la liturgie*, Paris, 1961, p. 739.
[2] Leo, *Sermones*, XII–XX, LXXV–LXXXI, LXXXVI–XCIV, P.L. LIV.
[3] *Liber Pontificalis*, ed. Duchesne, I, 141.

There is strong evidence that seasonal fasts at intervals during the year were of immemorial antiquity, and no authority gives us definite information about their institution. They were attributed to the Fathers (*Patres*) by St Leo;[1] and in the eleventh century by Bernold of Constance.[2] Egbert, Archbishop of York (732–67), speaks of them as being inaugurated by the Old Testament Fathers, and by apostolic teachers in the New Testament.[3] St Leo says they go back to the Apostles.[4] They were connected by St Leo and Egbert of York, as by *Liber Pontificalis*, with the seasonal harvest fasts of Zech. 8. 19. Thus St Leo says that the fast of the tenth month is not to be neglected because it was derived from Old Testament usage.[5] Egbert of York provides Old Testament quotations to show that each of the four seasons was prescribed in the Old Testament. The fast of the first month (March) is traced back to Moses;[6] that of the fourth month (June) to Moses also;[7] that of the seventh month (September) to Moses;[8] and that of the tenth month (December) to Jeremiah.[9]

There is a short anonymous tract preserved in three manuscripts of the ninth century, entitled *De obseruatione Quattuor Temporum*, edited by Dom G. Morin.[10] This traces the Lent Embertide back to Moses (Ex. 24. 18),[11] and also to Zech. 8. 19, altered to agree with Roman Embertides of the early Middle Ages;[12] the Pentecost Embertide to Deut. 16. 1, 10; the September season to 2 Esdras 8. 17—9. 3), and the

[1] Leo, *Serm.*, XVI, ii; P.L. 54, 177: sancti patres nostri diuinitus inspirati.

[2] *Micrologus*, XXIV; P.L. 151, 995.

[3] Egbert, *De institutione catholica dialogus*, XVI, P.L. 89, 440: quatuor temporum ieiunia patres instituerunt, secundum Dei legem, et nunc in Nouo Testamento sancti uiri atque apostolici doctores.

[4] Leo, *Serm.*, XX, i; P.L. 54, 189; *Serm.*, XCIII, iii; P.L. 54, 457.

[5] Leo, *Serm.*, XV, ii; P.L. 54, 175: decimi huius mensis solemne ieiunium quod non ideo negligendum est quia de obseruantia ueteris legis assumptum est; cf. Serm., XVII, i; P.L. 54, 180; *Serm.*, XX, i; P.L. 54, 188; *Serm.*, XCIII, iii; P.L. 54, 457.

[6] Ex. 3. 2; Deut. 11. 1.

[7] Deut. 26. 2.

[8] Lev. 23. 7.

[9] Jer. 56. 2. See *De inst. cath.*, xvi; P.L. 89, 440–2.

[10] "Notes liturgiques, 3: Un opuscule de l'époque carolingienne sur la raison d'être des Quatre-Temps", in *R.B.*, 30 (1913), pp. 231–4.

[11] Mense enim uerni temporis egressus es de Aegipto.

[12] Ipsum quoque primi mensis ieiunium dominus aliorumque trium temporum per Zachariam prophetam praecepit dicens: *Ieiunium primi*, Mar. ebd. I: *ieiunium IIIIti* Iun. secunda ebd.: *ieiunium septimi* Septembr. III ebd. *et ieiunium decimi* ebd. plena ante nat. domini *erit uobis in solemnitates praeclaras.*

But cf. the italicized words with Zech. 8. 19 in the Vulgate: Ieiunium quarti et ieiunium quinti et ieiunium septimi et ieiunium decimi erit domui Iuda in gaudium et laetitiam et in solemnitates praeclaras.

December season to Zech. 8. 19. The author is partly dependent upon Isidore of Seville.[1]

Ancient writers therefore see the origin of the Ember fasts in early Christian practice, perhaps apostolic, derived from Jewish practice as seen in the Old Testament. It is clear that nobody is certain about their exact origin, but that they are peculiarly Roman and go back to a remote antiquity. Certain modern writers have thought that they perhaps derive ultimately from pagan practice. Indeed, there are certain strong similarities between them and certain agricultural observances of pagan religion among the Romans, and it is of course quite possible that the Roman Church adopted and christianized an existing pagan observance.

Dom G. Morin enumerates striking resemblances between Ember Days and the *feriae* of the pagan Romans.[2] In the first place the *feriae* were not joyful feasts, but days of purification, to implore the blessing of the gods on the crops and to avert pestilence and ruin. Similarly, as we shall see,[3] the theme of the fruits of the earth is a primitive feature of Embertide liturgy, and has never been completely lost, although other thoughts and themes have come in. The Embertides of the Church still have a definite connection with the agricultural seasons of the year, both in their timing and in their subject-matter. They are also fasts and days of discipline, and not feasts. The three agricultural *feriae* of the Roman pagan Kalendar were the *Feriae sementinae*, *Feriae messis*, and *Feriae uindemiales*. The most important of the three to the Romans were the first, the *Feriae sementinae*. They were observed at the season of sowing, and are mentioned by Ovid, Varro, Pliny the Elder, and others. They ran from the setting of the Pleiades, on 11 November, to the winter solstice.[4] It is a curious but undoubted fact that in the earliest period of Roman liturgy the December Embertide was the most important, inasmuch as until Simplicius (468–83) ordinations at Rome were confined to the Saturday of the December Ember Week, and it was only after his time that other Embertides began to be used for the purpose of ordination. The *feriae sementinae* were not on a fixed date, but were a movable observance, of which the date was announced annually by the priests, and varied according

[1] Isidore, *De eccl. off.*, I, xxxix, 2; P.L. LXXXIII, 773–4.

[2] G. Morin, "L'origine des Quatre-Temps" in *R.B.*, 14 (1897), pp. 337–46.

[3] Chap. III, below, pp. 95–6.

[4] C. Plinius Secundus, *Nat. Hist.*, XVIII, 24, 56, ed. C. Mayhoff, Lipsiae, 1892, III, pp. 199–200.

to the earliness or lateness of the season and the state of the weather.[1] It will be noted at a later point that there was for a long time some variation in the dates of the Ember Weeks, and that the sermons of St Leo and the Sacramentaries give many examples of an official announcement of their observance, the *Denuntiatio Ieiunii*, proclaimed on the Sunday before the Ember Days.[2]

The *feriae messis* were observed between June and August, according to the locality and to the state of the crops. These were connected with the corn harvest, and correspond roughly in date to the summer Embertide. The autumn Embertide in September has its counterpart in the *Feriae uindemiales*, kept from the *Vinalia* on 19 August to the September equinox. This observance was connected with the grape harvest.

These three pagan observances seem to have some connection with the summer, autumn, and winter Embertides: they agree roughly in date, and they have an agricultural theme. There is nothing corresponding to the spring Embertide in Lent, but this Embertide was the last to be added by the Church: there were originally *Tria Tempora* and only later *Quattuor Tempora*, and the three original Embertides preserve agricultural references, which the liturgy of the Lent Ember Week does not.

The three most ancient Ember seasons, then, have preserved many references to the fruits of the earth, which may be considered in greater detail when we come to discuss the liturgy of Embertides.[3] But liturgical books retain other marks of a period devoted to thoughts of harvest. The Sunday Gospels in the period 10 August to 29 September (*post s. Laurentii*) in the seventh-century Gospel lists (which have remained more or less unchanged in the modern *Missale Romanum*) form a connected group, in which appears the theme of harvest, and also of healing and expulsion of demons, which are characteristic themes of the Ember seasons.[4] In the ancient Gospel lists may be noted the following:

Ebd. I post sc̄i Laurentii (=Pentecost XI). Mark 7. 31–7, the healing of a dumb man (Ephphatha).

Ebd. II post sc̄i Laurentii (=Pentecost XII). Luke 10. 23–7. The Good

[1] Ovid, *Fasti*, i. 657. [2] See pp. 76–8, below. [3] Below, pp. 95–6.

[4] See A. Chavasse, *Le sacramentaire gélasien*, pp. 461–9; "Les plus anciens types du lectionnaire et de l'antiphonaire romains de la messe", in *R.B.*, 62, Maredsous, 1952, pp. 59–61.

Samaritan. Note v. 34: *infudens oleum et uinum.* Oil and wine are two of the three characteristic Roman harvests.

Ebd. III post sci Laurentii (=Pentecost XIII). Luke 17. 11–19. Healing of the ten lepers.

Ebd. IV post sci Laurentii (=Pentecost XIV). Matt. 6. 24–33. "Be not anxious for your life, what ye shall eat, etc." . . . "Your heavenly Father knoweth that ye have need of all these things."

Ebd. V post sci Laurentii (=Pentecost XV). Luke 7. 11–16. The raising of the widow's son at Nain.

Ebd. I post sci Cypriani (= Pentecost XVI). Luke 14. 1–11. The curing of the palsied man and a meal with the Pharisees. Note v. 1, *manducare panem.*

The Communion chants of the same period are also a series, and are concerned with the harvest.[1] The first ten Sundays after Pentecost draw their communions from the psalms in numerical order, except for the ninth, of which the whole mass is out of place, thus:

Suns. after Pent.

I.	Ps. 9. 3.	VI.	Ps. 26. 6.
II.	Ps. 12. 6.	VII.	Ps. 30. 3.
III.	Ps. 16. 6.	VIII.	Ps. 33. 9.
IV.	Ps. 17. 3.	IX.	Matt. 6. 33.
V.	Ps. 26. 4.	X.	Ps. 50. 21.

From the eleventh to the fifteenth Sundays there is a complete break, and then the Psalm sequence resumes from the sixteenth Sunday onwards:

XVI. Ps. 70. 16–18.
XVII. Ps. 75. 12–13.
XVIII. Ps. 95. 8–9.
XIX. Ps. 118. 4–5.
XX. Ps. 118. 49–50.
XXI. Ps. 118. 81–4, 86.

The Communions of the Sundays from XI to XV are not part of this series, and are all concerned with the fruits of the earth.

I. *Dom. VI post nat. Apost.* (= Pent. XI).
Honora Dominum de tua substantia et de primitiis frugum tuarum, ut impleantur horrea tua saturitate et uino torcularia redundabunt. (Prov. 3. 9, 10.)

[1] See B. Capelle, "Antiennes pour la moisson dans le missel romain", in *Les Questions liturgiques et paroissiales*, XIV, Louvain, 1929, pp. 163–7.

II. *Dom. I post s. Laurentii* (= Pent. XII).
De fructu operum tuorum satiabitur terra ut educas panem de terra et uinum laetificet cor hominis et exhilaret faciem in oleo et panis cor hominis confirmet. (Ps. 103. 13–15.)
III. *Dom. II post s. Laurentii* (= Pent. XIII).
Panem de caelo dedisti nobis Domine habentem omne delectamentum et omnem saporem suauitatis. (Wisd. 16. 20.)
IV. *Dom. III post s. Laurentii* (= Pent. XIV).
Panis quem ego dedero caro mea est pro saeculi uita. (John 6. 52.)
V. *Dom. IV post s. Laurentii* (=Pent. XV).
Qui manducat carnem meam et bibit sanguinem meum in me manet et ego in eo, dicit Dominus. (John 6. 57.)

The sixth Sunday after the Apostles (29 June) is the Sunday before St Laurence (10 August), and falls therefore about 6 August, when, on the feast of St Sixtus, the *Hadrianum* provides for the blessing of grapes at mass. The references in the Communion (Prov. 3. 9, 10) to the offering of first-fruits, to the bursting barns and the overflowing wine-presses, are thoroughly apposite.

On the next Sunday (*Dom. I post s. Laurentii*) we have references to bread, wine, and oil, the three characteristic Roman harvests. After this the theme of bread is developed in a more spiritual fashion. On the Second Sunday after St Laurence we read of the bread from heaven, on the Third Sunday that this is the Body of Christ given for the life of the world, on the Fourth Sunday that to eat the flesh and drink the blood of Christ is to abide in him. Thus the series rises to a climax in speaking of the heavenly Eucharistic bread.

The other chants, apart from the Communions, in the Sunday masses of this period of the year do not appear to have any reference to the harvest.

There is no evidence to demonstrate conclusively the origin of the Ember seasons. It is clear from their propers even in the modern form that (except for the Lent Embertide) they have some connection with agricultural seasons; it may be significant that their dates coincide with the pagan *feriae*, not necessarily because the Embertides were the christianization of an existing pagan usage, but perhaps because the Roman Church took over Jewish observances of seed-time and harvest from the Old Testament, and applied them to the dates and circumstances of the Roman countryside. On the other hand, there would be nothing surprising in the suggestion that Ember Weeks are the old Roman pagan seasons invested with a Christian interpretation. This happened liturgically in other connections, for instance the fixing of our Lord's Nativity on 25 December, the *Natalis Solis Inuicti* of Mithraism; or of the Greater Rogation at Rome on 25 April, the day of the pagan *Robigalia*; or of the Roman feast of *Natale Petri de cathedra* on 22 February, replacing the *Cara cognatio*, a family festival.

Embertides go back to such an early period in Roman liturgical history that it cannot now be determined what their origin was. They were, however, for centuries confined to the City of Rome, and only spread gradually in the rites of Western Christendom as a whole, a process not completed before the twelfth century.[1]

The earliest references to Embertides are to *Tria Tempora* and not to *Quattuor Tempora*. They mention the fasts of the fourth, seventh, and tenth months, and the fast of the first month was a later addition. These three seasons are all connected with the harvest, but the fast of the first month, when it appears, has no reference to harvest, since there is no harvest at that time of the year. Thus *Liber Pontificalis*, of which the first edition dates from after 530, speaks of three fasts only, when it relates that St Callistus (218–25) instituted the Saturday fast at the harvests of corn, wine and oil:

> hic constituit ieiunium die sabbati ter in anno fieri frumenti uini et olei secundum prophetiam.[2]

Similarly the arrangement of the masses of the *Quattuor Tempora* in the Gelasian Sacramentary, which probably dates from about 560, betrays the fact that the fast of the first month is an addition, which was coming in about that time. In this Sacramentary the masses of the fast of the fourth month are embedded in the week of Pentecost, and are older than the Octave of Pentecost. Thus Gel. I, lxvi to lxxvi are concerned with the solemn baptisms on the Vigil of Pentecost. I, lxxvii contains the collects which go with the lessons of this Vigil. I, lxxviii and lxxix are Vigil masses of Pentecost. I, lxxx is the Mass of Pentecost, and I, lxxxi contains six evening prayers to be used in the Octave of Pentecost. There follows (I, lxxxii) the Notice or *Denuntiatio* of the fasts of the fourth, seventh and tenth months; lxxxiii contains the masses of the three Ember Days, Wednesday, Friday, and Saturday, and then follows (lxxxiv) the mass of the Octave Sunday. The evening prayers and the mass of the Octave Sunday are evidently later additions, but the Octave is not yet fully developed, since no masses are provided

[1] See pp. 68–72.

[2] *Liber Pontificalis*, I, 141.

for Monday, Tuesday, or Thursday. The notice of the impending fast, the *Denuntiatio*, is provided here for use at the fasts of the present fourth month, and of the seventh and tenth months. It is earlier than the institution of the fast of the first month, since it does not mention that fast, and, had it done so, would have been placed before the masses of that Ember Week, and not here at the head of the fast of the fourth month. It is a formula at least a hundred years old at the time of its insertion, since it is closely similar to the formula quoted by St Leo in many of his sermons at these fasts.[1]

The form and the position of the *Denuntiatio* in the Gelasian Sacramentary are relics of a time when there were only three such fasts. But in the earliest form in which this Sacramentary is now available, in ms. *Vaticanus Reginensis* 316, dating from about 750, the mass of the Saturday fast of the first month is placed at the end of the first week in Lent. We have in I, xviii the masses for this week, headed

ORATIONES ET PRAECES DOMINICA IN QUADRAGENSIMA INCOANTIS INICIUM

and providing for Sunday, Monday, Tuesday, Wednesday, Friday, and Saturday. These must be earlier than 715–31, when Gregory II instituted the Thursday masses in Lent. The following section (I, xix) is headed

> Iste orationes quae sequuntur prima sabbato in mense primo sunt dicendae.
> ORATIONES ET PRECES IN XII LECTIONES MENSE PRIMA.

Neither of these titles refers to Lent, but to the fast of the first month, and they are a manifest addition. The prayers which they introduce are the six collects which go with the six lessons of the Saturday Ember Vigil; and there is no provision for Ember Wednesday and Friday, as there is in this Sacramentary at the other three Embertides. These six collects are followed (I, xx–xxiv) by the prayers for the ordinations of priests, deacons, and subdeacons, and then at I, xxv the Lenten series resumes with the second Sunday in Lent.[2]

The compiler who arranged the section I, xix drew on the *Gelasianum* itself for the fifth and sixth prayers. He borrowed the text of the fifth prayer, *Da nobis obseruantiam*, from the *oratio super sindonem* of the third Wednesday in Lent,[3] and of the sixth, *Omnipotens sempiterne Deus, qui per continentiam*, from the second Friday in Lent.[4] The first and second

[1] See pp. 76–7, below. [2] See M. Andrieu, *Les Ordines Romani*, IV, p. 224.
[3] Ed. Mohlberg, No. 211. [4] Ibid., No. 184.

prayers of I, xix are derived from the Leonine,[1] but the third and fourth occur in no earlier source.[2] All these facts point clearly to the original Gelasian having provided in the early part of the sixth century for three Ember seasons only, those of the fourth, seventh, and tenth months.

It is difficult to be sure either when the fast of the first month came into existence, or when it was identified with the first week in Lent. About 600 in the original Gregorian Sacramentary and in the Würzburg Lectionary, the fast of the first month is identified with the first week of Lent, but this is clearly not the case in the original Gelasian Sacramentary, which makes provision for the first Saturday in Lent [3] and then gives the prayers for the Saturday of Twelve Lessons of the fast of the first month.[4] Thus the fast of the first month must have been instituted before 600, the date about which it was identified with first week of Lent.[5] Professor Chavasse gives reasons for dating the compilation of the Lenten arrangements of *Gelasianum* at about 560.[6]

A century earlier than this, St Leo (440–61) speaks of four annual fasts. At the December fast he mentions four seasonal fasts:

> Siquidem ieiunium uernum in Quadragesima, aestiuum in Pentecoste, autumnale in mense septimo, hiemale autem in hoc qui est decimus celebramus.[7]

In another sermon, delivered before the fast in September, he mentions four seasons without specifying them:

> Ideo enim ipsa continentiae obseruantia quattuor est assignata temporibus.[8]

The former text lists four fasts which divide into two groups. Those in Lent and Pentecost are attached to seasons of the liturgical year, and fasts observed at these times would not always be in the first and fourth months, though often they would be so. The other two are not placed in the liturgical year, but are in the seventh and tenth months of the civil year. The summer fast is definitely fixed by St Leo in the week of Pentecost, and Sermons 75–81, preached on the Sunday of Pentecost,

[1] Ed. Feltoe, 109, 7; 111, 13; ed. Mohlberg, Nos. 861, 878.
[2] A. Chavasse, *Le sacramentaire gélasien*, pp. 216–18.
[3] I, xviii, ed. Mohlberg, Nos. 129–33.
[4] I, xix, Nos. 134–9.
[5] See A. Chavasse, "Les messes quadragésimales du sacramentaire gélasien Vat. Reg. 316", in *E.L.*, LXIII, Rome, 1949, pp. 257–75.
[6] Ibid., p. 275.
[7] Leo, *Serm.*, XIX, ii; P.L. 54, 186.
[8] Leo, *Serm.*, XCIV, iii; P.L. 54, 459.

say that the fast is in the ensuing week, and give no hint that it is called the fast of the fourth month or attached to that month. At a later date it was in some places kept in the fourth month and detached from Pentecost.[1] The fast which occurs in Lent is not tied to the first week in Lent, as it was from the Gelasian Sacramentary onwards, nor to the first month, for if it fell early in Lent it would come in February as often as in March. What St Leo presents is a mixture of two systems which later crystallized into two distinct arrangements. One system is to have the Ember Fasts in the first, fourth, seventh, and tenth months of the civil year, which develops into the system later set forth by Amalarius and some of the Roman *Ordines*, according to which the fasts are in the first week of March, the second week of June, the third week of September, and the fourth week of December. The other is to integrate these fasts as far as possible into the liturgical year, having the first in the first week of Lent, the second in Pentecost Week, and the fourth in the third week of a four-week Advent; the third fast in September remaining in the third week of that month, since there is no ecclesiastical season to which to attach it. St Leo puts two fasts into periods of the ecclesiastical year, and two into fixed months. The spring fast in Lent is not by him fixed in the first week of Lent, and indeed it is doubtful whether it is distinguished at all as a period within Lent. He has several sermons delivered before each of the other three fasts, nine before the December fast;[2] seven before the Pentecost fast;[3] and nine before the September fast.[4] Many of these conclude with the customary announcement of the impending Ember Days.[5] None of his Lenten sermons contains this announcement, and none has special reference to a fast on Wednesday, Friday, and Saturday in the ensuing week. He seems to envisage the whole period of Lent as the fast, and not to have in mind a fast like the other three, fixed by official announcement on the preceding Sunday and confined to the three Ember Days. The probable conclusion is that the Lent Ember fast had not yet emerged in his day, but that it was emerging at Rome about the middle of the sixth century, when, about 560, the Lenten arrangements of *Gelasianum* were being drawn up. St Isidore of Seville, writing early in the seventh century, long before Embertides had been introduced into Spain,

[1] See pp. 68–72, below.
[2] Leo, *Serm.*, XII–XX; P.L. LIV.
[3] Leo, *Serm.*, LXXV–LXXXI; P.L. LIV.
[4] Leo, *Serm.*, LXXXVI–XCIV; P.L. LIV.
[5] E.g. *Serm.*, XIII, XV, XVI, XVII, XVIII, XIX, LXXV, LXXVI, LXXVIII, LXXXI, LXXXVI, LXXXVIII, LXXXIX, XC, XCII, XCIV.

speaks of several fasts, of which the first is Lent;[1] the second after Pentecost;[2] and the third on 10 September.[3]

The development of the fast of the first month may indeed be traced by comparing the rubric in the third book of the Gelasian [4] at the end of the Canon of the Mass, which provides for the announcement of the forthcoming Ember Days to be made between the *Pax* and the Communion, together with the formula for this announcement given in the first book,[5] with Formula VI of *Liber Diurnus*, which was composed at the end of the seventh century.[6] The Gelasian rubric says:

> Post haec commonenda est plebs pro ieiunii quarti septimi et decimi mensis temporibus suis. . . .

The title of the text of this announcement, which is placed immediately before the forms for the fast of the fourth months, is:

> DENUNTIATIO IEIUNIORUM QUARTI SEPTIMI ET DECIMI MENSIS

Liber Diurnus says in Formula VI:

> Ordinationes uero presbiterorum seu diaconorum non nisi *primi* quarti septimi et decimi mensium ieiuniis sed et ingresso quadragesimali atque mediane uespere sabbati nouerit celebrandas.[7]

This formula, based on a text of Gelasius,[8] has been emended by the addition of the word *primi*, for in the letter of Gelasius the first month was not mentioned. It was therefore added to this text between 496, the date of the death of Gelasius, and the end of the seventh century, but its establishment before St Gregory, with other considerations, suggests a date about 560. As it is not mentioned in the first edition of *Liber Pontificalis* (after 530) it must date from between 530 and 590.[9]

From then onwards there were four Ember Weeks. As long as there were three, they had agricultural reference, and were connected from the time of their institution with the harvests of corn, wine, and oil in June, September, and December. This connection with harvest has left its mark to this day on the liturgy of Ember Days. But gradually ordinations came to be conferred at the Embertides. This must be

[1] S. Isidorus Hispalensis Episcopus, *De ecclesiasticis officiis*, I, 37; P.L. 83, 773–4.
[2] Ibid., I, 38. [3] Ibid., I, 39. [4] III, xvi, ed. Mohlberg No. 1260.
[5] I, lxxxii, ed. Mohlberg No. 652.
[6] R. J. Hesbert, *Antiphonale Missarum Sextuplex*, p. lxix, n. 4.
[7] Ed. Sickel, p. 6. [8] Ed. Thiel, *Ep. Rom. Pontif.*, p. 368.
[9] A. Chavasse, "Messes quadragésimales du sacramentaire gélasien", in *E.L.*, 63, Rome, 1949, pp. 260–1.

discussed in greater detail in a subsequent chapter,[1] but certainly the Ember seasons were among those used by St Gelasius for ordinations. In earlier times ordinations at Rome had been confined to the Saturday Vigil of the December Ember Week, but when it became necessary and usual to confer them at other times, it began perhaps to be felt that an ordination day was desirable in the long gap of six months between December and June. This may have led to the institution of the Ember fast in March or in Lent. There is no definite evidence to prove this, but it seems a likely explanation of the addition of a fourth seasonal fast which has and can have no reference to harvest, and there is nothing to contradict it.

A recent lecture by Fr Jose Janini [2] seeks to establish that Pope Siricius (384–98) introduced at Rome the four seasonal Ember fasts, as a counterblast to the heresy of Jovinian, and before 391. Siricius is assumed to have compiled an inaugural mass of the Pentecost Ember season which now survives scattered about the Verona Sacramentary.[3] These texts seem to have been arbitrarily selected and arranged in this order to suit the argument. It is asserted on the authority of St Philaster of Brescia that the four Embertides existed in 391, when he published the *De haeresibus*. In *De haeresibus* 149 [4] Philaster mentions four annual fasts:

> Nam per annum quatuor ieiunia in Ecclesia celebrantur; in Natali primum, deinde in Pascha, tertium in Epiphania, quartum in Pentecoste. Nam in Natali Saluatoris Domini ieiunandum est, deinde in Paschae Quadragesima, atque in Ascensione itidem in caelum post Pascha die quadragesimo, inde usque ad Pentecosten diebus decem: id quod postea fecerunt beati apostoli post Ascensionem ieiuniis et orationibus insistentes . . .

It by no means follows that because an author mentions four fasts he must mean the four Embertides. Fifty years after Siricius St Leo speaks of four fasts, but the first of these is Lent and not an Embertide, for it is clear that the Lent Embertide did not appear until long after Leo, and even longer, therefore, after Siricius. But none of the four fasts mentioned by Philaster occurs at the right time of the year to be an Embertide. Not one of them is in the time of any harvest, and they are all confined to the first half of the ecclesiastical year. The first is in the Christmas season, the second in the forty days between Easter and the Ascension, the third (out of order) in Epiphany, and the fourth in

[1] Pp. 78–84, below. [2] *S. Siricio y las cuatro temporas*, Valencia, 1958.
[3] Ed. Mohlberg, Nos. 226, 206, 227, 207, 229. [4] P.L. XII, 1286–7.

Pentecost, which, as we see from the next sentence, does not mean in the week or octave of Pentecost, which certainly did not exist in Philaster's time, but in the fifty days of Eastertide, which is a frequent meaning of the term "Pentecost" when this term is not applied to the actual fiftieth day after Easter. Indeed, as we see from the apostolic precedent which Philaster cites, this fourth fast occurs in the days between Ascension and Pentecost, that is between the fortieth and fiftieth days after Easter.

At a later date far-fetched explanations began to be invented to explain why there were four Ember seasons. Thus we are told by Amalarius, who died about 850, that the four seasons of the year by their respective delights draw us away from love of the Creator, and so it is fitting that each season should have a seasonal fast to recall us to the service of God. Likewise the four parts of the day, morning, noontide, evening, and night, tempt us away from God, and demand four annual fasts to recall us to him. Each such fast has three days, as each season of the year has three months, and we require one day's fast for each of the months, which the Ember Days provide.[1] In Egbert of York we find this explanation slightly amplified. The world consists of four parts, North, South, East, and West; man of four elements, fire, air, water, and earth; there are four cardinal virtues, prudence, temperance, fortitude, and justice; there were four rivers flowing out of Paradise, which are a type of the four Gospels; there are four seasons of the year, and in every respect four is a perfect number, and therefore there are four seasonal fasts.[2] The argument from the four seasons and three months in each is found in Pseudo-Alcuin.[3] Bernon of Reichenau, who died in 1048, reproduces the explanation of Egbert of York, and adds that the particular days of Wednesday, Friday, and Saturday are chosen because Wednesday was the day when the Jews plotted to kill Christ, Friday the day on which they carried this into effect, and Saturday because on that day the Apostles mourned his death.[4]

[1] Amalarius, *De ecclesiasticis officiis*, II, ii; P.L. 105, 1076 ff.; ed. Hanssens, II, 202–4; cf. Ps. Alcuinus, *De diuinis officiis*, XXVIII; P.L. 101, 1227.

[2] Egbert, *De institutione catholica*, XVI; P.L. 89, 440–2.

[3] *De diu. off.*, XXIX; P.L. 101, 1228.

[4] Berno, *Libellus de quibusdam rebus ad missae officium pertinentibus*, VII; P.L. 142, 1073–1080; *Dialogus qualiter Quatuor Temporum Ieiunia per sua sabbata sint obseruanda*, P.L. 142, 1087–98.

2. *The Four Embertides*

I. THE LENT EMBERTIDE

This is certainly the latest of the four Ember seasons to be instituted. It was evidently not observed about 530, when the first edition of *Liber Pontificalis* was drawn up, which mentions the institution of the Saturday fast at the other Embertides by Callistus, but is silent about an Embertide in the spring. By the end of the sixth century, the time of St Gregory the Great, it had been instituted, and is known to the Roman Epistolary of Würzburg (600–25), to the Gospel Book of Würzburg (650), and to the later lectionaries, such as the *Comes* of Murbach and that of Alcuin in the eighth century. We have seen that the fast of the first month had been instituted about 560, and at any rate in the period 530–600. But when instituted it was not tied to Lent. It was the fast of the first month, March, and observed always in that month, whenever Lent fell. Thus Formula VI of *Liber Diurnus*, which is probably earlier than St Gregory I, speaks of ordinations of priests and deacons at the fasts of the first, fourth, seventh, and tenth months, and also at the beginning and in the middle of Lent.[1] The evidence of the Gelasian Sacramentary [2] shows that about the period 560–90, that is between the institution of the Lent Embertide and the time of St Gregory, this Embertide was not necessarily observed in the first week of Lent. It was fixed in the first week of March, and so could fall in Sexagesima Week, or in any subsequent week up to the fourth week of Lent inclusive. Thus by the end of the sixth century three ordinations were possible in the spring very close together, on the first Saturday of March, and the first and fourth Saturdays of Lent. Three ordination days so close together were not needed, and the first reduction was to suppress ordinations in the first week of Lent, but to keep the other two days. *Ordo Romanus* XV, which was compiled to serve with a sacramentary of Gelasian type, and which goes back to a time earlier than St Gregory, notes that there were no ordinations on the first Saturday in Lent unless this happened to be the first Saturday of

[1] Quoted above, p. 61.

[2] I, xviii and xix; see p. 58, above.

March.[1] The Gallicanized *Ordo* XXXVII B, of the eighth or ninth century, still fixes the fast of the first month in the first week of March.[2] *Ordo* XV says that the first Saturday of Lent and the Saturday of the fast of the first month have each twelve lessons, even if they do not coincide.[3] The spring Embertide is observed in March according to *Ordo* XVII, 6;[4] *Ordo* XXXVII A. 1;[5] *Ordo* XXXVII B, 1;[6] B 7 (mss. JQ);[7] *Ordo* XXXVIII, 1.[8] Many of these *ordines* define the time of the ordination as the sixth hour on Saturday.

The Pope, however, had some discretion in respect of the date to be chosen for this Ember Week. If the first week in Lent occurs in March, we read in *Ordo* XV, 84,[9] according to MSS. G and W, priests are ordained; but if not, the ordinations are held in the next week or the

[1] *Ordo* XV, 84, ed. Andrieu, III, pp. 115–16: Prima uero ebdomada in quadragissima, IIIIta et VI feria et sabbato, staciones publicas faciunt et ieiunium et XII lectionis in ipso sabbato consumantur. Et si fuerit ipso sabbato de marcio mense ordinationis sacerdotum faciunt. Sin autem in alia ebdomada uel tercia, quando pontifex iudicauerit iterum IIIIta et VIta feria celebrare uidentur; sicut prius et sabbato duodecim lectionis legunt et ordinantur qui ordinandi sunt G; Inde uero prima ebdomada in quadragesima, iterum quarta et sexta feria seu et sabbatum stationes publicas faciunt et ieiunium cum XII lectionibus in ipso sabbato consummantur. Et si fuerit ipsum sabbatum de martio mense ordinationes sacerdotum faciunt. Sin autem in alia ebdomada uel tertia quando pontifex iudicauerit iterum IIIIta et VIta feria seu et sabbatum cum XII lectionibus sicut prius celebrare uidentur et ordinantur qui ordinandi sunt M; In XLma uero prima ebdomada, si in mense martio uenerit, IIII et VI feria seu et sabbato omnes publicas stationes faciunt ad sanctum Petrum in XII lectionibus. Sin autem minime in martio mense prima ebdomada uenerit, in alia uel tertia ebdomada quando pontifex iudicauerit, XII lectiones agendae sunt W.

[2] *Ordo* XXXVII B, 1, ed. Andrieu IV, p. 249: In primo mense quarta et sexta feria uel sabbato in prima ebdomada de mense primo (HT) (mensis ipsius GJMQ; *om.* EFL) primum ieiunium celebretur (celebratur EFJLQ); XXXVII B, 7; ed. Andrieu IV, p. 250: et hic est ordo de quattuor temporibus quomodo officium missae peragatur: Mense martio prima sabbati hora VI JQ; XXXVII B, 16, ed. Andrieu IV, p. 254: in mense martio erit celebratio XII lectionum I sabbati . . . GM.

[3] *Ordo* XV, 84, ed. Andrieu III, pp. 115–16, quoted in note 1 above.

[4] *Ordo* XVII, 6, ed. Andrieu III, p. 176: In ipsa autem ordinatione sacerdotum preter quattuor tempora anni nullatenus ordinatur: id est primum uer, quod est ebdomada prima mensis primi marcii, ita tamen si ipsa ebdomata infra quadragisima contigerit . . .

[5] *Ordo* XXXVII A, 1, ed. Andrieu IV, p. 235: In primo mense, a quarta et sexta feria uel sabbato in prima ebdomada de mense primo, primum ieiunium celebretur.

[6] *Ordo* XXXVII B, 1, ed. Andrieu IV, p. 249: quoted above, note 2.

[7] *Ordo* XXXVII B, 7, ed. Andrieu IV, p. 250: quoted above, note 2.

[8] *Ordo* XXXVIII, 1, ed. Andrieu IV, p. 267: mense martio prima sabbati hora sexta.

[9] Ed. Andrieu, III, p. 115; quoted above, n. 1.

next week but one, according to the pontiff's discretion.[1] *Ordo* XVII, of the end of the eighth century, on the other hand, says that the spring Embertide is in the first week of March, even if this falls in Lent.[2] The first week of Lent is also an ordination week, but the pontiff has the right to move this by one week or by two.[3]

In the *Hadrianum* and the *Paduense* the Ember masses are placed in the first week of Lent, and as the descent of these two manuscripts is different, their agreement on this point seems to indicate that the arrangement that the spring Ember Week is the first week of Lent goes back to St Gregory himself, and that it was he who fixed it in this week, whereas for some thirty years before him, since its introduction, it had been kept in the first week of March without reference to Lent. Ember Week is placed in the first week of Lent in other Roman documents, for example the eighth-century Antiphonary and the *Comes* of Würzburg, representing Roman use at the beginning of the seventh century, just after St Gregory. It was introduced into England by Roman missionaries, and so Archbishop Egbert claims that England derived from St Gregory through St Augustine the practice of keeping Ember Days in the first week of Lent, and apparently this practice has always been maintained in England.[4] This is a further indication that it was St Gregory who fixed the spring Embertide in this week.

Roman usage was introduced by St Augustine into England, but was not always fully understood in other countries outside Rome, and the Frankish Empire often followed the original Roman usage of observing the spring Embertide in the first week of March, and not necessarily in Lent at all. Amalarius, writing to Hilduin, Abbot of St Denys, about 825,[5] had long thought that the Ember fasts were in

[1] "quando pontifex iudicauerit".

[2] *Ordo* XVII, 6; ed. Andrieu, III, p. 176, quoted on p. 65, n. 4.

[3] *Ordo* XVII, 88, ed. Andrieu, III, p. 187: Inde uero prima ebdomata in quadraginsima iterum quarta et sexta feria seu et sabbatum stationes publicas faciunt et ieiunium cum XII lectiones in ipso sabbato consumantur. Et si fuerit ipsud sabbatum de martio mense ordinationem sacerdotum faciunt. Si autem in alia ebdomata uel tertia quando pontifex iudicauerit iterum quarta et sexta feria seu et sabbatum cum duodecim lectionibus, sicut prius, celebrare uidentur. Et ordinantur qui ordinandi sunt.

[4] Egbert, *De instit. cath.*, XVI, i; P.L. 89, 440: Quod ieiunium (*sc.* uernum) sancti patres in prima hebdomada mensis primi statuerunt, quarta et sexta feria et sabbato, exceptis diebus quadragesimalibus. Nos autem in Ecclesia Anglorum idem primi mensis ieiunium, ut noster didascalus beatus Gregorius in suo antiphonario et missali libro per paedagogum nostrum beatum Augustinum transmisit ordinatum et rescriptum, indifferenter de prima hebdomada quadragesimae seruamus.

[5] Amalarius, *Ep. ad Hilduinum abbatem*, 7, ed. Hanssens I, p. 342.

the first, fourth, seventh, and tenth months, since this form of title was primitive. So in his *Liber Officialis* [1] he had included this rule, and said that the ordinations should be held on the first Saturday in March, the second Saturday in June, the third Saturday in September, and the Saturday before the Nativity in December. He had learned at Constantinople in 813 or 814 from Peter, Abbot of Nomentola, that this was not the case, and that at Rome the spring Embertide was in the first week of Lent, and not the first week of March.

Amalarius had originally learned his Roman liturgy from Frankish sources, and in this matter Frankish use was to observe the first week in March as Ember Week. The Council of Seligenstadt in 1022 gave detailed rules for fixing the Ember Weeks, and as regards the March Ember Week it says that if 1 March falls between Sunday and Wednesday, then that same week is Ember Week; if 1 March fall on Thursday, Friday, or Saturday, Ember Week is the following week.[2] Bernon of Reichenau, who died in 1048, expounds the same method of computation, and says that it should never be observed in February, but always wholly within March, between the fourth and the tenth.[3] The Frankish rule is also enunciated by the Council of Rouen in 1072. As late as 1222 the Council of Oxford [4] was supporting the Frankish rule, but the Roman rule triumphed and has been since observed. It was established by Gregory VII in 1078, who affirmed the Gregorian rule of keeping the first week of Lent as Ember Week, and attacked the Gallican rule as an innovation.[5] This was reiterated by Urban II in 1095, and appears in liturgists, including Bernold of Constance.[6]

[1] Amalarius, *De eccl. off.*, I, i, 10–13; P.L. 105, 1076; ed. Hanssens II, pp. 200–1.

[2] Conc. Salingunstadiense, a. 1022, can. II, Mansi, *Concilia*, XIX, 396–7; De incerto autem ieiunio quatuor temporum hanc certitudinem statuimus, ut si kalendae Martii in quarta feria siue antea euenerint, eadem hebdomada ieiunium celebretur. Si autem kalendae Martii in quintam feriam aut sextam aut sabbatum distenduntur, in sequentem hebdomadam ieiunium differatur.

[3] Berno, *Libellus de quibusdam rebus ad missae officium pertinentibus*, VII; P.L. 142, 1075–6; *Dialogus qualiter Quatuor Temporum Ieiunia per sua sabbata sint obseruanda*, P.L. 142, 1092–3.

[4] Canon VIII, in Mansi, *Concilia*, XXII, 1154.

[5] Licet noua consuetudo aecclesiae nulla fulta auctoritate numeret inter ieiunia et ordinationes quatuor temporum primam ebdomadam primi mensis Martis et secundam quarti, id est Iunii, uetus tamen auctoritas sanctorum patrum constituit, ut in initio quadragesimali et in ebdomada pentecostes debeant obseruari; quoted in Andrieu IV, p. 217.

[6] *Micrologus*, XXIV; P.L. 151, 995: Gregorius papa septimus . . . constituit ut ieiunium quod dicitur Martii in prima ebdomada quadragesimae omni anno celebretur. On the date of the Embertides see Andrieu IV, pp. 213–32.

2. THE PENTECOST EMBERTIDE

There were similarly divergent traditions about the date of the fast of the fourth month, and it was disputed for a long time whether it should be observed in June, the fourth month, or in the week immediately following the Day of Pentecost, which of course might fall in May.

The week of Pentecost is now the Octave of Pentecost, a replica of Easter Week, and an Ember Week. The oldest of these three is the Ember Week, though before it was an Ember Week it was doubtless an ordinary ferial week, with fasts on Wednesday and Friday, which were a resumption of the weekly stational fasts after the seven-week interruption of the unbroken joy of Eastertide, which concluded with the great Octave Sunday of Pentecost. An Ember Week immediately followed Pentecost, and it is called the fast of the fourth month from at least the time of Gelasius, and this title appears in the Leonine and Gelasian Sacramentaries, and in the old Neapolitan Gospel Book.

The original Roman rule was to observe Ember Week in the week of Pentecost, in spite of the title of the fast of the fourth month (June). In the older Gospel Books it is assumed that the fast of the fourth month comes in this week. The stations on Wednesday, Friday, and Saturday are those belonging to an Embertide. On Saturday there are twelve lessons.[1] Earlier than these Gospel Books, St Leo speaks of the summer fast in Pentecost.[2] This is quoted by Bernold of Constance in the *Micrologus*, which claims it as authority for confining the summer Embertide to the week of Pentecost.[3] Egbert of York refers to the offering of the first-fruits in the Old Testament, and to the saying of our Lord about fasting when the Bridegroom is taken away, and argues that it is fitting after the close of the Paschal cycle to have a fast in the second week of the fourth month. St Gregory transmitted to the Church of England by the hand of St Augustine, and in the antiphonary and missal attributed to him, the tradition of observing this fast in the week of Pentecost.[4]

[1] See W. H. Frere, *Studies in Early Roman Liturgy*, II, pp. 124–5.

[2] *Serm.*, XIX, 2; P.L. LIV, 186: aestiuum in pentecoste.

[3] *Micrologus*, XXV; P.L. 151, 999: Ubi euidentissime indicauit ieiunium quarti mensis non nisi in hebdomada Pentecostes esse celebrandum. Si enim istud in Iunio mense, sicut autumnale in Septembri, semper ieiunandum decerneretur, non minus Iunium quam Septembrem nominare posset. Ergo iuxta sententiam huius apostolici, sicut autumnale semper in Septembri, ita aestiuum in Pentecoste semper debeamus celebrare.

[4] Egbert, *De instit. cath.*, XVI, ii; P.L. 89, 440.

The Gelasian Sacramentary also fixes it in this week. It has no masses in the week of Pentecost, except the three for the Ember Days, which are placed between Pentecost and its octave day.[1] This is not accidental, for it is commented on in the preface of Wednesday, where we have the phrase *post illos enim laetitiae dies* borrowed from a Leonine mass in the fast of the fourth month,[2] which is dependent upon St Leo.[3] In the *Hadrianum* the Ember masses are placed similarly in the week of Pentecost, and this is true also of *Paduense*. The Gregorian tradition is thus fixed, since these two Gregorian books have different lines of descent, and their agreement in this matter points to the arrangement of the Ember Week in Pentecost (as indeed to the arrangement of the other Ember Weeks in the first week of Lent, between 16 and 27 September, and after the third Sunday in Advent) going back to St Gregory himself, as Egbert of York testifies in respect of the Pentecost fast.[4] As late as the third quarter of the eighth century *Ordo* XVI [5] fixes the summer Embertide in the week of Pentecost, and likewise *Ordo* XVII.[6]

Up to the middle of the seventh century the Sunday after Pentecost was vacant, as usual after Ember Days, since its mass was the vigil mass of Saturday night, with the ordinations. About that time the vacant Sunday was provided with a mass, and became the Octave Day of Pentecost. The *Gelasianum* registers this stage in the development of the week of Pentecost. I, lxxx is the mass of Pentecost, and is followed by the evening prayers within the Octave of Pentecost, six in number,[7] and then by the *Denuntiatio* of the Ember fast,[8] and the masses for the three Ember Days,[9] which have no reference to the Holy Spirit. After this comes the mass of the Octave Day of Pentecost,[10] which appears to be ancient, since it possesses two collects, a *super sindonem*, and an *oratio ad populum*. *Gelasianum* provides no masses for the weekdays of Pentecost week except for Wednesday, Friday, and Saturday.

When once the *vacat* Sunday was filled up, it soon came to be regarded as the Octave of Pentecost, and this octave was established at Rome about 630–50. Thursday remained an aliturgical day till the eighth century, but the other five days were provided with masses, and this was done at one time. The subject of them is the Holy Spirit. This arrangement is seen in the Gregorian Sacramentary (both

[1] *Gel.*, I, lxxxiii. [2] Ed. Feltoe, p. 28; ed. Mohlberg, p. 29, No. 229.
[3] *Serm.*, LXXVIII, i, 3; P.L. 54, 417.
[4] Egbert, *De instit. cath.*, XVI, 2; P.L. 89, 441.
[5] *Ordo* XVI, 51, ed. Andrieu III, p. 154.
[6] *Ordo* XVII, 6, ed. Andrieu III, p. 176.
[7] I, lxxxi. [8] I, lxxxii. [9] I, lxxxiii. [10] I, lxxxiv.

Hadrianum and *Paduense*), in the Antiphonary, and in the Roman Gospel Books of the seventh and eighth centuries.[1]

So long as Pentecost had no octave, but was the concluding day of the joyful Paschal cycle, it was natural to recur to fasting in that week, after the seven weeks of Eastertide which had been completely free of fasts. When once Pentecost had an octave, this octave was modelled on the octave of Easter, and naturally it began to be regarded as inconvenient to observe a solemn fast in the midst of a joyful octave. So from the second half of the seventh century, after the establishment of the octave of Pentecost, there was a tendency to move the Ember Days out of this week, and a divergence sprang up between Roman and Gallican practice in this respect, as it did in respect of the spring fast. The Gallican practice was to observe Ember Week in one of the three weeks following that of Pentecost. Sometimes it was kept in June, being the fast of the fourth month. The old rule, as stated by Bernold of Constance, was to keep it in the second week of June.[2] In 683 Pope Leo II ordained nine priests and three deacons on 27 June, which was the Saturday of the third week after Pentecost, Pentecost in that year falling on 7 June. This does not appear to have been an ordination *extra quattuor tempora*, and, if not, it points to the postponement of the Ember Week.[3] According to *Ordo* XXXV,[4] dating from the beginning of the tenth century, the candidates must be ordained on Ember Saturday, but the Pope is at liberty to fix Ember Week anywhere within its own month.

The *Comes* of Würzburg, representing Roman use at the beginning of the seventh century, places the summer Ember Days in the second week after Pentecost, and the *Comes* of Murbach, of the end of the eighth century, in the week after that, the week of the third Sunday after Pentecost; and this is their position in the eighth-century Gelasians, except Angoulême.[5] The Council of Mayence in 813 maintained that Roman tradition fixed this Ember Week in the second week of June,[6] and this is supported by Rabanus Maurus, writing between 813 and

[1] A. Chavasse, *Le sacramentaire gélasien*, pp. 247–52.

[2] *Micrologus*, XXV; P.L. 151, 999.

[3] *Liber Pontificalis*, I, pp. 360 and 362, n. 11.

[4] *Ordo* XXXV, A, 15, ed. Andrieu, IV, p. 36; cf. Hesbert, *Antiphonale*, pp. lxviii–lxxi, and G. Morin, in *R.B.*, 27 (1910), pp. 58 ff.

[5] See L. Brou, "Étude historique sur les oraisons des dimanches après la Pentecôte dans la tradition romaine", in *Sacris Erudiri*, II, 1949, pp. 203, 207.

[6] Conc. Moguntinense, can. XXXIV, in M. G. H., Concil. II, 269, cited in Andrieu, IV, p. 214.

826,[1] and by Raoul of Bourges (841–68).[2] The Council of Seligenstadt, in 1022, gives detailed rules for fixing the Ember Weeks, and says that if the result of the application of these rules is the concurrence of Ember Saturday with the Vigil of Pentecost, Ember Week is postponed for a week.[3] This Frankish method of reckoning is found also in Bernon of Reichenau.[4]

It is clearly undesirable to have Ember Week in the week before Pentecost, since the ordinations would then fall at the Vigil service of Pentecost, which was appropriated to the solemn baptisms. If this Vigil falls in May, the Ember Days will be *tempore suo*, that is in June. The station of Whitsun Eve was at St John Lateran, where baptism was administered, from immemorial antiquity, whereas the Ember Saturdays with their ordinations had the station always at St Peter's. *Ordo* XXXVII A regulates this carefully.[5]

Amalarius testifies that the summer Ember Week was not always observed in the octave of Pentecost.[6] Coincidence with Pentecost was therefore possible, but not normal, and Amalarius was familiar with the Frankish rule of observing the second Saturday in June as the ordination day, which can coincide with Whit-Saturday when Easter is late. Otherwise the Embertide would be observed a week or two after Pentecost. Amalarius maintains the rule that there are fourteen weeks between Embertides, and if so the spring Embertide, if observed in the first week of March, would fix the summer Embertide in the second week of June.[7] This arrangement is also seen in the Pontifical.[8] The eighth-century Gelasians put it in the week following the third Sunday after Pentecost.

The divergence between the Roman tradition of the week of Pentecost and the Gallican tradition of some later week persisted for some centuries, but it was finally settled by Gregory VII (1073–85) and Urban II, who established the Roman rule. Gregory VII attacked the

[1] Rabanus Maurus, *De instititione clericorum*, II, 24, cited in Andrieu, IV, p. 215, n. 1.

[2] Rodulfi *Capitula* XXX; P.L. 119, 718, cited in Andrieu, IV, p. 215, n. 2.

[3] Conc. Saligunstadiense, can. II, cited in Andrieu IV, p. 216.

[4] P.L. 142, 1095–6.

[5] *Ordo* XXXVII A, 12, ed. Andrieu IV, pp. 237–8; and Andrieu's comment on IV, pp. 228–30.

[6] Amalarius, *De eccl. off.*, II, i, 2; P.L. 105, 1073, Hanssens, II, p. 197: In temporibus quando agimus XII lectiones solemus ieiunare etiamsi prouenerint in octauis Pentecostes.

[7] *Micrologus*, XXV; P.L. 151, 997.

[8] *Ordo* L, xiv, ed. Andrieu, V, p. 101.

Gallican use as an innovation, and recalled the Church to the original use, of the week of Pentecost.[1] This was reiterated by Urban II in 1095, and by councils and liturgists, including Bernold of Constance,[2] who cites the authority of Leo I and Gregory I, and of the Sacramentary and Antiphonary. As late as 1222, however, the Council of Oxford held to the Frankish rule, but the Roman rule triumphed and has since been observed.

3. THE SEPTEMBER EMBERTIDE

The proper of this Embertide is placed in the Gelasian Sacramentary in the *Sanctorale* [3] between 29 September (St Michael) and 7 October (SS. Marcellus and Apuleius): in other words it is not placed where it is actually observed, but at the end of the *Sanctorale* for September. There is some evidence that before St Gregory this Embertide was observed at Rome in the first week of September. The oldest liturgical documents are divided about the reckoning of the Sundays after Pentecost. Both systems reckon them in small groups, and not in a continuous series, as now: *post Pentecosten*, *post Apostolos* and so on. Some, however, reckon *post s. Cypriani* (14 September) and some *post s. Angeli* (29 September). Baumstark suggested that this division derived from divergent traditions about the date of the September Ember Days. The new series of Sundays is reckoned after the Ember Week, which is over before 14 September if it is in the first full week of September, and before 29 September if it is in the third week. The Gregorian Sacramentary has on the first Sunday of September the title *Mensis septimi orationes. Die dominico ad sanctum Petrum.* St Peter's is always the station on the Sunday before the Ember Days.[4] The second Sunday of September in this Sacramentary is the vacant Sunday after the Ember Days. Those documents which reckon *post s. Cypriani* have the Sunday before Embertide between the 1st and the 7th; and the vacant Sunday between the 8th and the 14th. Those which reckon *post s. Angeli* have the Sunday before Embertide on the third Sunday in September (15th to 21st) and the vacant Sunday 22nd to 28th. The consecration of St Gregory was on Sunday, 3 September 590, in the Basilica of St Peter. If this were the Sunday before the Ember Days the station would in any case have been at St Peter's, and it was the Roman practice to consecrate Bishops of Rome at St Peter's. It is to be noted

[1] Cited above, p. 67, n. 5.
[2] *Micrologus*, XXV; P.L. 151, 997.
[3] II, lx.
[4] See pp. 75–6, below.

that the Secret and Preface of the Gregorian mass *Pro natali papae* on the anniversary of his consecration are related to those of the Sunday before the September Embertide, and have similarities also with the writings of St Gregory, and it may well be that this mass was the work of St Gregory himself, compiled for his own consecration.[1]

There is no later evidence for the observance of Ember Week in the first week of the month, and the uniform tradition after St Gregory is to observe it in the third week of the month, after St Cyprian on the 14th. In the Gospel and Epistle Books compiled after the time of St Gregory the Great, the mass of the Sunday before the September fast has the title *Ebd. I mensis septimi*. It opened the second series of sixteen masses in the period after Pentecost, and fell between 13 and 19 September.

A number of the *Ordines* prescribe the third week in September for the Ember Days.[2] Egbert of York says that Ember Week is the week before the autumnal equinox, whether it be the third week or not.[3] Bernold of Constance states that the autumn Embertide is observed in the seventh month, but not so rigidly fixed as the others to a particular week. It was by his time the only seasonal fast not fixed in a particular week of the ecclesiastical year, the others being fixed in the first week of Lent, the week of Pentecost, and the third week of Advent. But, as he states, the custom was that the September Ember Week included the third Saturday of September.[4] *Missale Romanum* now fixes the Ember Days on the Wednesday, Friday, and Saturday *post Festum Exaltationis sanctae crucis*, that is, after 14 September.

4. THE DECEMBER EMBERTIDE

The masses of the three Ember Days in December are placed in the Gelasian Sacramentary at the end of Book II, which contains the *Sanctorale* concluding with St Thomas on 21 December.[5] This is followed by a Common of Saints, with eight masses, and then by five

[1] L. Brou, "Étude historique sur les oraisons des dimanches après la Pentecôte dans la tradition romaine", in *Sacris Erudiri*, II, 1949, pp. 123–223, especially pp. 183–6.

[2] E.g. *Ordo* XVII, 6, ed. Andrieu III, p. 176; *Ordo* XXXVII A, 3, ed. Andrieu IV, p. 235; *Ordo* XXXVII B, 3, ed. Andrieu IV, p. 249; XXXVII B, 7, ed. Andrieu IV, p. 250; XXXVII B, 16, ed. Andrieu IV, p. 254; *Ordo* XXXVIII, 1, ed. Andrieu IV, p. 267; *Ordo* L, xiv, 3, ed. Andrieu V, p. 101.

[3] Egbertus, *De instit. cath.*, XVI, iii; P.L. 89, 442.

[4] *Micrologus*, XXVI; P.L. 151, 1000.

[5] II, lxviii.

Sunday masses for Advent.[1] Finally come the three Ember Days,[2] and Book II then concludes with the colophon *Explicit Liber secundus de nataliciis sanctorum martirum.* The texts of these masses in *Gelasianum* remain largely what they were before the introduction of Advent, and show little accommodation to the Advent themes.[3]

The Roman tradition was to observe this Embertide in the third week of a four-Sunday Advent, so that the ordinations fell on the day before the fourth Sunday, and this is uniform in the whole tradition and down to the present day. But in the eighth century it is expressed rather differently from this. *Ordo Romanus* XV, usually entitled *Capitulare ecclesiastici ordinis,* contains liturgical notes and ordinances of all kinds, arranged according to the ecclesiastical year, and beginning with Advent. Its date is about 750. The Sunday before Christmas Day is the Conception of St Mary, an early equivalent of the Annunciation in non-Roman churches. It occurs in all the Mozarabic books, and the Council of Toledo in 686 fixes it on 18 December. In the Ambrosian rite the Sunday is entitled *de exceptato* and is the Sunday before Christmas, as in *Ordo* XV.[4] The Ember Days fall in the week following.[5] But this can only happen in a full week, giving room for the three Ember fasts and the ordinations on the Saturday evening. *Ordo* XV, 5 [6] provides that if this Saturday is the Vigil of Christmas the Ember Week will be pushed back one week. This manner of expressing the situation is found also in *Ordo* XVI, 18–21, in the third quarter of the eighth century,[7] and in *Ordo* XVII, 3–5, which is the *Breuiarium ecclesiastici ordinis,* composed at the end of the eighth century, and more or less copied from *Ordines* XVI and XVII.[8] Similar provisions are made in *Ordines* XXXVII A, 4 [9] and XXXVII B, 4 [10] and 16;[11] and they are mentioned by Bernon of Reichenau [12] and Egbert of York,[13] who says that the Ember Days fall in the last full week before Christmas.

[1] II, lxxx–lxxxiv.

[2] II, lxxxv.

[3] T. Maertens, "L'avent" in *Mélanges de science religieuse,* 18, Lille, 1961, pp. 47–110; A. Chavasse, "L'avent romain du VIe au VIIIe siècle", in *E.L.,* 67 (1953), pp. 297–308.

[4] *Ordo* XV, 2, ed. Andrieu III, p. 95: Deinde una dominica ante natale Domini, incipiunt canire de concepcione sanctae Mariae.

[5] *Ordo* XV, 3, ed. Andrieu, III, p. 96: In ipsa uero ebdomata quarta et sexta feria seu et sabbatum stationis puplicas faciunt . . .

[6] Ed. Andrieu III, p. 96.

[7] Ed. Andrieu III, pp. 149–50.

[8] Ed. Andrieu, III, pp. 175–6.

[9] Ed. Andrieu, IV, p. 235.

[10] Ed. Andrieu, IV, p. 250.

[11] Ed. Andrieu, IV, p. 254.

[12] *Libellus de quibusdam rebus ad missae officium pertinentibus,* VII, P.L. 142, 1076.

[13] *De instit. cath.,* XVI, iv; P.L. 89, 442.

By the time of Bernold of Constance in the eleventh century the feast of St Mary on 18 December has disappeared, and the *Micrologus* does not mention it, but speaks of the Ember Days as falling in the third week of Advent. He retains, however, the rule that if the Vigil of Christmas comes on a Saturday, the ordinations are on the previous Saturday, and therefore the Ember Days in the previous week, for the Vigil mass and the Ordination or Ember Saturday mass cannot coincide. He further provides that if St Thomas (a feast as old as *Gelasianum*) occurs on an Ember Day, there are two masses, one at 9 a.m. for St Thomas, sung with *Gloria in excelsis*, and one after noon for the Ember Fast, without *Gloria*.[1]

3. *The Liturgy of the Ember Days*

A. THE STATIONS

The Roman Missal still retains notes of a station at St Peter's on the third Sunday in Advent and on the Day of Pentecost, both of which are Sundays before Ember Weeks. This station on these days can be traced back to the Gregorian Sacramentary, in which also there is a title after 16 September

MENSIS SEPTIMI ORATIONES DIE DOMINICO AD SANCTUM PETRUM.

This is followed by the masses of that Sunday and the Wednesday, Friday, and Saturday following, in Ember Week, and then the mass supplied for the *vacat* Sunday following.[2] As this occurs in both *Paduense* and *Hadrianum*, it must go back to the original *Gregorianum*. So three of the four Sundays before Ember Weeks had at least from the time of the original Gregorian Sacramentary the same station, at St Peter's. It cannot be established from the Sacramentaries that this station went back any earlier, since the Gelasian Sacramentary has no note of stations, being a presbyteral book for use in the *tituli*, and not a papal sacramentary, and the *Leonianum* likewise does not mention stations. The station of the first Sunday in Lent, however, is not at

[1] *Micrologus*, LVIII; P.L. 151, 1019.

[2] Ed. Lietzmann, No. 163.

St Peter, but at St John Lateran, as in all the Antiphonaries.[1] But as this Embertide was the latest of the four, and was not originally fixed in the first week of Lent, it would appear that when it was established the station of the first Sunday in Lent, already an important day, which was already fixed at St John Lateran by the end of the fourth century, was not altered to bring it into conformity with the newly established Ember Week. So we are entitled to conclude that normally there is a tradition that the station on the Sunday before the Ember Days is at St Peter.[2]

At this mass the forthcoming Ember Days were announced. The Leonine Sacramentary has preserved two examples of the text of this announcement:[3]

ADMONITIO IEIUNII MENSIS SEPTIMI ET ORATIONES ET PRECES
Annua nobis est, dilectissimi, ieiuniorum celebranda festiuitas, quam mensis septimi sollemnis recursus indicit. Quarta igitur et sexta feria succedente solitis eandem conuentibus exsequamur, sabbatorum die hic sacras acturi uigilias ut per obseruantiam competentem Domino purificatis mentibus supplicantes beatissimo Petro apostolo suffragante et praesentibus periculis exui mereamur pariter et futuris. per.[4]

INVITATIO PLEBIS IN IEIUNIO MENSIS DECIMI[5]
Hac hebdomade nobis mensis decimi sunt recensenda ieiunia. quapropter fidem uestrae dilectionis hortamur ut eadem quarta et sexta feria solitis processionibus exsequentes sabbatorum die hic ipsum uigiliis sollemnibus expleamus quatenus apostolicis suffragantibus meritis propitiationem Dei nostri perseuerantiam debitae seruitutis obtineat. per.[6]

These announcements both refer to the fasts of the ensuing Wednesday, Friday, and Saturday, and to the fact that the station on Saturday for the solemn vigil service at which holy orders were conferred was, as on the previous Sunday, at St Peter's. In the former announcement the Saturday station is here (*hic*), in the latter *hic ipsum* (at this same place), and each refers to the apostolic merits or intercession of St Peter, the

[1] Ed. Hesbert, No. 40a.

[2] See L. Brou, "Une ancienne station romaine à Saint-Pierre pour le dimanche précédant les Quatre-Temps", in *E.L.*, 60, Rome, 1946, pp. 143–50; and "Étude historique sur les oraisons des dimanches après la Pentecôte dans la tradition romaine", in *Sacris Erudiri*, II, 1949, pp. 162–6 and 182.

[3] See *D.A.C.L.*, art. "Annonce des fêtes", by F. Cabrol, I, cols. 2230–2241.

[4] Ed. Feltoe, pp. 108–9; ed. Mohlberg, *Sacramentarium Veronense*, Rerum Eccles. Documenta, Series Maior, Fontes, I, Rome, 1956, p. 108 (No. 860).

[5] This is out of place under September.

[6] Ed. Feltoe, p. 144; ed. Mohlberg, p. 114, No. 905.

patron. Many of St Leo's sermons on Ember Days conclude with a similar admonition or notice,[1] which is doubtless not his invention, but an already stereotyped liturgical formula, which must thus date from earlier than the middle of the fifth century.[2] A common form of the announcement in Leo is:

> Quarta igitur et sexta feria ieiunemus, sabbato autem apud beatum Petrum uigilemus.

Instead of *hic ipsum* in the *Inuitatio plebis in ieiunio mensis decimi* quoted above, he says[3] either *in idipsum*, which may possibly be a corruption of *hic ipsum*; or else *pariter*, which means "here, as we are now, at St Peter's".[4] In one sermon before the December Embertide he says:

> Quarta igitur et sexta feria ieiunemus: sabbato autem apud praesentem beatissimum apostolum Petrum uigilias celebremus.[5]

The word *praesentem* fixes the station of the previous Sunday and of the ordination Saturday at St Peter's, and this tradition is established by the time of St Leo and remains constant.

The Gelasian Sacramentary has similar announcements in two alternative forms for impending Ember Days in the fourth, seventh, and tenth months, but none for the first month. They are placed together before the masses of the Pentecost Ember Days.[6] The first refers to the Saturday station at St Peter's, but not the second.

The manuscripts BCKS of the Antiphonary specify the station of the third Sunday in Advent as *ad sanctum Petrum*;[7] RBKS say that the station of Pentecost is there,[8] but no mention is made of the station in September, on the seventeenth Sunday after Pentecost, which in these manuscripts precedes the Ember Days in autumn.

This announcement of the Ember Days was made at mass, after the *Pax Domini*. There is in the Gelasian Sacramentary a rubric in the Canon of the Mass which makes provision for this.[9] After *Pax Domini sit semper uobiscum* and the response, it reads:

[1] *Serm.*, XIII, XV, XVI, XVII, XVIII, XIX, LXXV, LXXVI, LXXVIII, LXXXI, LXXXVI, LXXXVIII, LXXXIX, XC, XCII, XCIV, P.L. LIV.

[2] See F. L. Cross, "Pre-Leonine elements in the Proper of the Roman Mass", in *J.T.S.*, 50, Oxford, 1949, pp. 191–7.

[3] *Serm.*, LXXV, i, 6; P.L. 54, 403.

[4] *Serm.*, XIII; P.L. 54, 173; LXXXVI, ii; P.L. 54, 418; LXXXVIII, v; P.L. 54, 444.

[5] *Serm.*, XVI, v; P.L. 54, 179.

[6] I, lxxxii, ed. Mohlberg, Nos. 652–3.

[7] Ed. Hesbert, No. 4.

[8] Ed. Hesbert, No. 106.

[9] Ed. Mohlberg, III, xvii, No. 1260.

Post haec commonenda est plebs pro ieiunii quarti septimi et decimi mensis temporibus suis, siue pro scrutiniis uel aurium apertionum, siue orandum pro infirmis uel adnuntiandum natalitia sanctorum. Post haec communicat sacerdos cum ordinibus sacris cum omni populo.

The stations of the Ember Days are fixed in the whole of the ancient tradition, and show no variation. The station on Ember Wednesdays at all four seasons is *ad sanctum Mariam Maiorem*, on the Fridays *ad sanctos Apostolos*, and on the Saturdays *ad sanctum Petrum*. No single authority contradicts this arrangement, though *Ordo* XV mistakenly describes the Apostles' Church used on Friday as that of the Apostles James and John.[1] There was no basilica at Rome of this dedication, and the Church of the Apostles where the Ember Friday stations were fixed is that of SS. Philip and James at the foot of the Quirinal.[2] The Saturday station at St Peter's is frequently mentioned in the Sermons of St Leo, and this station was therefore as old as the middle of the fifth century. The Gelasian Sacramentary likewise mentions only the Saturday station,[3] as does *Ordo* XXXVII A, 12.[4] The ancient manuscripts of the Antiphonary consistently give the three stations of these days at all the seasons.[5] The ancient Epistle and Gospel Books also note the same stations.[6]

B. ORDINATIONS

There was a rule as ancient as the third century at Rome that bishops must be consecrated on Sunday,[7] and this is laid down in the *Apostolic Tradition* of Hippolytus.[8] But consecrations are not confined to the Ember seasons; they may take place on any Sunday in the year.[9] *Ordo* XXXVI is a Gallicanized *Ordo* with a Roman base, dating from the end of the ninth century. Likewise it was the ancient rule, which has always been maintained in Roman tradition, that the orders of priest

[1] *Ordo* XV, 3, ed. Andrieu III, p. 96; and see Andrieu's note, p. 60, par. 3.
[2] *Liber Pontificalis* I, 306.
[3] I, lxxxii, ed. Mohlberg, No. 652.
[4] Ed. Andrieu, IV, p. 237.
[5] Ed. Hesbert, Nos. 5-7; 43, 45, 46; 109–11; 190–2.
[6] Frere, II, Nos. 64, 66, 67; 140–2; 229–31; 269–71; III, Nos. 29, 31, 32; 97, 98, 98a; 126–8; 143–5; G. Morin, "Evangiles de Würzburg", in *R.B.*, 28, pp. 302, 307, 315.
[7] C. H. Turner, "The Papal Chronology of the third century, 3, Antiquity of the rule of Sunday ordination", in *J.T.S.*, 17, Oxford, 1916, pp. 341 ff.
[8] Ed. Dix, p. 3; ed. Botte, p. 27.
[9] Cf. *Ordo* XXXVI, 29, ed. Andrieu, IV, p. 200: episcopi autem omni tempore benedicuntur.

and deacon are conferred on Sundays. St Leo, who is the first to state this rule, says that it is agreed that Sunday begins liturgically on Saturday evening:

> Quod ergo a patribus nostris propensiore cura nouimus esse seruatum, a uobis quoque uolumus custodiri, ut non passim diebus omnibus sacerdotalis uel leuitica ordinatio celebretur, sed post diem sabbati, eius noctis quae in prima sabbati lucescit exordia deligantur, in quibus his qui consecrandi sunt ieiuniis et a ieiunantibus sacra benedictio conferatur. Quod eiusdem obseruantiae erit, si mane ipso dominico die, continuato sabbati ieiunio, celebretur, a quo tempore praecedentis noctis initia non recedunt, quam ad diem resurrectionis, sicut etiam in pascha domini declaratur, pertinere non dubium est . . . ut his qui consecrandi sunt numquam benedictio nisi in die resurrectionis dominicae tribuatur, cui a uespera sabbati initium constat ascribi.[1]

And again:

> legitimo die . . . die sabbati uespere quod lucescit in prima sabbati uel ipso die dominico.[2]

St Leo objected to ordinations on any other day.[3] Evidently he contemplated ordinations on any Sunday, but St Gelasius, fifty years later, restricts them to the fasts of the fourth, seventh, and tenth months, the beginning of Lent, and *mediana* week.

> Ordinationes uero presbyterorum seu diaconorum non nisi quarti septimi uel decimi mensium ieiuniis, sed et in ingressu quadragesimali atque medianae uespere sabbati nouerit celebrandas.[4]

This constitution was repeated in *Liber Diurnus* with the addition of the first month, *primi* being inserted before *quarti*.[5] According to this rule there can be six ordinations in the year, three of them very close together in the spring, one in the fast of the first month, one in the first and one in the fourth week of Lent. Later they were restricted to the four Ember Weeks.[6]

Originally the orders of deacon and priest were conferred on these stated days, at the vigil mass of the night of Saturday to Sunday. This is the only mass of Saturday, and the proper chants and prayers

[1] *Ep.* IX, 1; P.L. 54, 625–6.
[2] *Ep.* X, 6; P.L. 54, 634.
[3] *Ep.* VI, 6; P.L. 54, 620; *Ep.* CXI; P.L. 54, 1021.
[4] *Gel.*, *Ep.* XV, 3, in Thiel, *Ep. Rom. Pontif.*, I, p. 380.
[5] *Liber Diurnus*, Formula VI, ed. Sickel, p. 6.
[6] *Ordo* XVII, 6, ed. Andrieu, III, p. 176: in ipsa autem ordinatione sacerdotum preter quattuor tempora anni nullatenus ordinatur.

appointed in the Sacramentaries and Antiphonaries, which will be considered in the next chapter, are used at this mass. Sunday had no other mass except the ordination mass, and so is marked in most of the ancient authorities *Dies dominica uacat*. In churches where there was no ordination, this Sunday would require a mass, and so later it was supplied with one, drawn usually from the propers of the preceding Ember Days, especially from Wednesday and Saturday.[1] Furthermore, a tendency developed to anticipate the vigil mass for reasons of convenience, so that, instead of beginning late on Saturday night and running on into the early hours of Sunday, it was celebrated on Saturday evening, or else in the afternoon of Saturday. *Ordo* XXXV, 15, in the first half of the tenth century, appoints 2 p.m. (*hora diei octaua*) as the time for this mass.[2] The Romano-German Pontifical brings it back to Saturday morning at 9 a.m.,[3] or leaves it to the Bishop's discretion.

To the end of the eighth century Rome on the whole preferred to confer orders at the December Embertide. If we can rely on *Liber Pontificalis*, ordinations at Rome were confined to December until the second half of the fifth century. Simplicius (468–83) was the first to depart from this custom, and he was followed by Gelasius I (492–6). Simplicius began to ordain in the Lent Embertide, in February,[4] and between then and the end of the eighth century eleven popes out of forty-eight conferred orders at times other than December, namely Gelasius I,[5] Symmachus,[6] Felix IV,[7] Gregory I,[8] Leo II,[9] Sergius I,[10] Gregory II,[11] Zacharias,[12] Stephen II,[13] and Adrian II.[14] St Gregory the Great was the first Pope to ordain in September;[15] Simplicius, Gelasius, and Symmachus also ordained in February, and Felix IV in February and March. Ordinations in December are mentioned in *Ordo* XV, 4;[16] *Ordo* XVI, 20;[17] and *Ordo* XVII, 4;[18] and in Lent in *Ordo* XV, 84[19] and *Ordo* XVII, 88.[20]

The conferment of minor orders was not confined to any particular day until the time of the Frankish Sacramentaries, in the tenth century, which put them on Ember Saturdays. Previously they could be con-

[1] See p. 83, below. [2] Ed. Andrieu, IV, p. 36.
[3] *Ordo* L, xv, 2, ed. Andrieu V, p. 103. This is taken from *Ordo* XXXVI A, 5, ed. Andrieu, IV, p. 236.
[4] *Liber Pontificalis*, I, 249. [5] Ibid., I, 255. [6] Ibid., I, 263. [7] Ibid., I, 279.
[8] Ibid., I, 312. [9] Ibid., I, 360. [10] Ibid., I, 376. [11] Ibid., I, 410.
[12] Ibid., I, 435. [13] Ibid., I, 456. [14] Ibid., I, 514. [15] Ibid., I, 312.
[16] Ed. Andrieu, III, 96. [17] Ibid., III, 150. [18] Ibid., III, 176.
[19] Ibid., III, 115–16. [20] Ibid., III, 187.

ferred at any time or place,[1] while the orders of deacon or priest could only be conferred at the public ordinations.[2]

The rites for the ordination of priests and deacons are inserted in the Gelasian Sacramentary at the end of the first week in Lent. After the masses of Sunday, Monday, Tuesday, Wednesday, Friday, and Saturday of this week,[3] come the prayers for the first Saturday in the first month,[4] and then the ordination services, with rubrics.[5] After this follows the proper of the second Sunday in Lent.[6] The section I, xx–xxiv is a Romano-Gallican addition to the original *Gelasianum*, and was compiled in Gaul at the end of the seventh or the beginning of the eighth century; but most of its prayers are Roman and occur in the Leonine Sacramentary or in the Gregorian *Hadrianum*: the rest are Gallican.[7]

The ceremonies preliminary to ordination are described in *Gel.* I, xx,[8] and in *Ordines Romani* XXXIV, XXXVI, and XXXIX.[9] The first of these is purely Roman, the second and third Roman with Gallican additions. The candidates for the diaconate and priesthood appeared before the Pope on Monday in Ember Week, and stated on oath that they had not committed any of the four grievous crimes which were an impediment to holy orders:[10]

> Primitus enim secunda feria in ebdomada quando XII lectiones debent fieri, uocat pontifex electos et iurant ante eum super reliquias sanctorum, adstante primicereo et secundicerio et archidiacono et archipresbitero et cui uoluerit, de IIII capitula quod canones prohibent.[11]

On the Wednesday of this week the *collecta* is at St Adrian, and the station at St Mary Major:

[1] *Ordo* XXXVI, 3, ed. Andrieu, IV, p. 195.

[2] Ibid., 4. cf. *Ordo* XXXV, 14, ed. Andrieu IV, p. 36: Subdiaconum uero uel ceteros gradus inferiores consuetudinem habet sedes apostolica consecrandos die dominico uel ceteris festiuitatibus preclaris, in quibus pontifici conplacuerit uel quo tempore ipse missarum sollemnia agere uoluerit. Nam presbiterum et diaconum nullatenus consecrat nisi in quattuor tempora, ordine quo inscribendum est ulterius.

[3] *Gel.*, I, xviii, ed. Mohlberg, Nos. 104–33.

[4] I, xix, ed. Mohlberg, Nos. 134–9.

[5] I, xx–xxiv, ed. Mohlberg, Nos. 140–62.

[6] I, xxv, ed. Mohlberg, Nos. 163–7.

[7] A. Chavasse, *Le sacramentaire gélasien*, pp. 5–27.

[8] Ed. Mohlberg, Nos. 140–2.

[9] Ed. Andrieu, III, pp. 603 ff.; IV, pp. 195 ff.; 283 ff.

[10] See Andrieu, IV, p. 274.

[11] *Ordo* XXXIX, 1, ed. Andrieu, IV, p. 283.

Fit enim conuentus populi et congregatio regionum primum ad sanctum Adrianum et inde pergit pontifex una cum populo precedente solito apparatu id est cruces turibula uel tale, usque ad sanctam Mariam ad presepem.[1]

At St Mary Major, before the Epistle, the candidates stood in the *presbyterium* and a reader read out their names and invited objections: this reader was not a *lector* in the ordinary liturgical sense, but, as we see from *Ordo* XXXIX, 5 [2] a *scriniarius*, or archivist of the Papal chancery.[3] The formula used by him was:

In nomine domini nostri Iesu Christi, si igitur est aliquis qui contra hos uiros aliquid scit de causa criminis, absque dubitatione exeat et dicat; tanto memento communionis suae.[4]

A slightly fuller form is provided in *Ordo* XXXVI, 9:

Cognoscat fraternitas uestra quia Ille et Ille aduocantur in tali uel tali officio. Si quis habet contra hos uiros aliquam quaerellam exeat confidenter propter Deum et secundum Deum et dicat. Memor sit tamen omnino communionis suae.[5]

This procedure of *si quis* was repeated on Friday at the Holy Apostles.[6] On Saturday at the Vigil mass at St Peter's, at which the ordination took place, the usual pattern of Ember Saturday masses was followed. After the Epistle and the Tract, the candidates stood in the *presbyterium* and the Pope called them by name in turn:

Talis presbyter, regionis tertiae titulo tale, Ille.[7]

A deacon presented the candidates for the diaconate, and they were ordained,[8] and then the candidates for the priesthood were presented and ordained.[9] The newly ordained priests gave the kiss of peace to the bishops and the priests, and then took their places with the college of priests,[10] and made their offering and communicated. They then received a consecrated host, from which they communicated for the next forty days.[11] The newly ordained priests then rode on horseback to their titles, where they celebrated mass, assisted each by a senior

[1] *Ordo* XXXVI, 5, ed. Andrieu, IV, p. 196.
[2] Ed. Andrieu, IV, p. 283.
[3] See Andrieu, IV, p. 275.
[4] *Ordo* XXXIX, 5, ed. Andrieu, IV, p. 283.
[5] Ed. Andrieu, IV, p. 196.
[6] *Ordo* XXXVI, 12, ed. Andrieu, IV, p. 197; *Ordo* XXXIX, 10, ed. Andrieu, IV, p. 284.
[7] *Ordo* XXXIX, 10, ed. Andrieu, IV, p. 284.
[8] *Ordo* XXXIX, 20, ed. Andrieu, IV, p. 284.
[9] *Ordo* XXXIX, 23, ed. Andrieu, IV, p. 285.
[10] *Ordo* XXXIX, 24, ed. Andrieu, IV, p. 285.
[11] *Ordo* XXXIX, 25, ed. Andrieu, IV, p. 285.

priest, who also acted as Gospeller; and at this mass they had the right to use *Gloria in excelsis*, which thereafter would for them be restricted to Easter.[1]

The Gelasian Sacramentary has only one election and *si quis*, and places this on Saturday.[2] It also places the ordination at a different point in the mass. In *Ordines* XXXVI and XXXIX the election is after the Tract which follows the Epistle; but in *Gelasianum* (*Vat. Reg.* 316) it is after the first prayer which follows the Introit.[3] This is, however, the position in which it comes in *Ordo* XXXIX on Wednesday and Friday. The election is followed by an interval, and then comes the ordination Litany, beginning with *Kyrie eleison*,[4] after which the ordination takes place. This is an error, arising from the suppression of the elections of Wednesday and Friday, and the conflation of their arrangements with those of Saturday.[5]

The Sundays after Ember Weeks were originally vacant, and marked *Dominica Vacat*, or the like, in the liturgical books. The ordination mass during Saturday night to Sunday morning was the Sunday mass, and no further provision was necessary for Sunday. Later there was need for a mass on Sunday, at any rate in those churches which had no ordinations, and masses began to be supplied, often made up of texts repeated from ferias of the Ember Week, especially of Wednesday and Saturday.[6] This process was complete by the early years of the seventh century.

The title *Dominica uacat* often survived after the day had in fact been provided with a mass, for example in the Gregorian Sacramentary.[7] The treatment of this Sunday in the Antiphonaries varies. At the Advent Embertide [8] MBK leave the Sunday blank; R entitles it *Dominica I ante natale Domini*, and provides a mass; S calls it *Dominica quarta* (sc. *Aduentus*) and provides a mass; and C has the title *Dominica uacat*, but provides it with a mass. In the Lent Embertide [9] MBCKS have a blank, with the note *Dominica Vacat*; R has *Dominica in XL^ma^ Item ad missam sicut iam supra scriptum est in Sabbato*. The Sunday after the Pentecost Embertide is not mentioned at all in any of the manuscripts, with either a title or a mass: they all proceed from Ember Saturday to the June *Sanctorale*. In September there is no evidence

[1] *Ordo* XXXIX, 26–8, ed. Andrieu, IV, p. 285.
[2] I, xx, ed. Mohlberg, No. 141.
[3] Ed. Mohlberg, No. 140.
[4] I, xx, ed. Mohlberg, No. 142.
[5] A. Chavasse, *Le sacramentaire gélasien*, pp. 23, 26.
[6] *Micrologus*, XXIX; P.L. 151, 1002–3.
[7] Ed. Lietzmann, Nos. 45, 118, 167.
[8] Ed. Hesbert, No. 7 bis.
[9] Ed. Hesbert, No. 46 bis.

from C, which has a lacuna; and the others all have a mass *Ebdomada* (or *Dominica*) *XVIII post Pentecosten* (or *post octabas Pentecosten*), and none of them marks it as vacant.

C. THE LITURGY OF EMBER DAYS

i. GENERAL SHAPE

The framework is the same at all the four seasons, but the content of the prayers, chants, and lessons varies a good deal. Prayer and fasting in general are their main themes, which recur at all four seasons, and penitence is frequently mentioned, and in the Gospels the expulsion of demons is a characteristic subject.

The order of the lessons differs amongst the three Ember Days at each season. Wednesday has almost always two lessons before the Gospel, and therefore two Graduals to follow them. Friday, on the other hand, has lost one of these lessons, and retains only one lesson before the Gospel. Saturday, like the vigils of Easter and Pentecost, has twelve lessons, and is usually called *Sabbatum in XII lectionibus*.

The two lessons on Wednesday are always from the Old Testament.[1] Each is normally followed by a Gradual. All the six early manuscripts of the Antiphonary provide two graduals on Wednesday in the Lent Embertide,[2] and so do four of them on Wednesday in the Advent Embertide,[3] though here M and R provide only one, which seems to be an error. Yet in the September Embertide no manuscript provides more than one,[4] nor on the Wednesday in Pentecost.[5] The Wednesday in *mediana* week, which shares many characteristics with the Ember Weeks,[6] still preserves two Old Testament lessons before the Gospel in the Roman Missal.[7] Bernon of Reichenau, who died in 1048, explains that there are two lessons on Wednesdays in Ember Weeks to warn the ordinands that they should have knowledge of the law and the prophets.[8] This is a fanciful argument, for in no case do the ancient lessons in this mass come from the Law and the Prophets respectively.

[1] Frere, *Studies in Early Roman Liturgy*, III, Alcuin Club Collections XXXII, Oxford, 1935, Nos. 29, 97, 126, 143.

[2] Ed. Hesbert, No. 43a. [3] Ibid., No. 5a. [4] Ibid., No. 190.

[5] Ibid., No. 109.

[6] See below, pp. 101–4.

[7] Feria quarta post Dominicam iv Quadragesimae.

[8] *Libellus de quibusdam rebus ad missae officium pertinentibus*, VII, P.L. 142, 1075: ut hi qui in sabbato sunt consecrandi admoneantur ut notitiam legis et prophetarum habeant.

The proper of the Advent Embertide has been reconstructed, but at the other three seasons the Offertory *Meditabor*, from Psalm 118. 47–8, 57–9, recurs on the Wednesdays.[1] It speaks of fidelity to God's commandments.

Unlike Wednesday and Saturday, Friday, the least important of the three Ember Days, has only one lesson before the Gospel. In the most ancient Epistolaries it is always a prophetic lesson, and never from the Law or the New Testament, and it varies at each season. There is therefore only one Gradual and only one Collect on these Fridays. Bernon explains this one lesson as illustrating the fact that the Law and the Prophets are recapitulated in one Gospel.[2] The Offertory on this day is constant, except in Advent: it is Psalm 102. 2, 5b; 39. 4, 7b–19,[3] which praises God for his benefits, and speaks of pardon and love for those who keep his commandments.

The solemn liturgy of the Vigil on Saturday evening is the most developed of the three Ember Day masses, and it has similarities with the great Paschal and Pentecostal Vigils. In no document has it more than six lessons, excluding the Gospel, but its title is constantly *Sabbatum in duodecim lectionibus*. It had, in fact, six lessons, but originally in the Byzantine period of Roman history (550–750) the lessons were each read in Greek and Latin, and this accounts for the number twelve which survived in the title of this office long after the Greek lessons had disappeared.[4] In accordance with the six lessons the Sacramentaries provide six collects, and the Antiphonaries six chants. The six collects in the Gelasian and Gregorian Sacramentaries cannot have been chosen before the seventh century. The sixth Collect in September and December,

> Deus, qui tribus pueris mitigasti flammas igneas, concede, quaesumus, ut nos famulos tuos non exurat flamma uiciorum.[5]

or the sixth in Pentecost, which is styled ITEM POST BENEDICTIONEM as is No. 1174,

[1] Ed. Hesbert, Nos. 43, 109, 190.

[2] *Libellus de quibusdam rebus* . . . P.L. 142, 1075: quia lex et prophetia in uno euangelio recapitulatur.

[3] Hesbert, Nos. 45a, 110a, 191.

[4] Amalarius, *De eccles. off.* II, i,l; P.L. 105, 1073; Hanssens II, p. 197; *Micrologus*, XXVIII; P.L. 151, 1002: hoc autem sabbatum quamuis sex lectiones tantum habeat, dicitur tamen XII lectionum, eo quod antiquitus eaedem lectiones bis legebantur, Graece scilicet et Latine.

[5] Ed. Mohlberg, Nos. 1049 and 1174.

Deus, cuius adorandae potentiam maiestatis flamma seuientes incendium sanctis tribus pueris in splendore demutatum est animarum, aecclesiae tuae similibus adesto remediis, ut de grauioribus mundi huius aduersitatibus propitiatione caelesti populus tuus ereptus exultet.[1]

implies that the fifth lesson, which immediately precedes it, is the cento from Daniel 3. The sixth prayer at the Lenten Embertide is different.[2] The Roman Epistolary of Alcuin has this lesson, but it is a recent addition, and is missing from Alcuin in September, and is not present in the Epistolary of Würzburg, which contains intact the old Roman system of lessons. The first five lessons are from the Old Testament, and the sixth lesson is the Epistle: these make the twelve lessons, and the Gospel is separate and additional.

The usual number of chants provided by the Antiphonaries for Ember Saturdays is six, comprising four Graduals, the *Benedictiones*, and the Tract; but they do not always give the text of the graduals in full, but perhaps only one, two, or three of them. None of the manuscripts mention the *Benedictiones* in December, and not always at the other Embertides. Only the Compiègne Antiphonary gives their full text, and that in Lent. They were a sort of extension of the fifth lesson, drawn from Daniel 3 like the lesson, and the lesson and *Benedictiones* are sometimes called in the old books *Lectio cum cantico*, probably both read by the reader in different tones. The sixth collect in the Sacramentaries is usually *Deus qui tribus pueris*, and, if not, another collect referring to the three Holy Children, such as the sixth collect at Pentecost in the Gelasian, quoted above. The Daniel lesson is a cento from Daniel 3. 49–50a, 47–8, 50b–51, and the *Benedictus* is from Daniel 3. 52–5; Ps. 103. 3; Daniel 3. 58 (57), 59 (74, 78), 79. The prayer which usually follows, *Deus qui tribus pueris*, occurs in both the Gelasian and Gregorian Sacramentaries.

Certain other features are common to the four Ember seasons. For instance, the Tract on Saturday, from Psalm 116, occurs in Lent and September.[3] The Offertory *Meditabor*[4] is common to Ember Wednesday in Lent, Pentecost, and September; *Domine Deus salutis* is common to Ember Saturday in the same seasons,[5] and *Benedic anima* is the Offertory of Friday in Lent and September.[6]

[1] Ed. Mohlberg, No. 671. [2] Ibid., No. 139. [3] Ed. Hesbert, Nos. 46a, 192.
[4] Ibid., Nos. 43a, 109, 190. [5] Ibid., 46a, 111, 192. [6] Ibid., 45a, 191.

ii. PARTICULAR SEASONS

a. December. The masses of the December fast in the Gelasian Sacramentary [1] are archaic in form, unlike those of the later Gregorian form which this Sacramentary has in September.[2] All three days have an *Ad populum* at the end of the Mass.[3] There is, however, one anomaly, namely that there are three prayers before the Secret on Friday, and two only on Wednesday, instead of the other way about, which we should expect, as there are in this week, as in other Ember Weeks, two lessons before the Gospel on Wednesday, but only one on Friday. The lessons of Wednesday are Isaiah 2. 2–5, and Isaiah 7. 11–15;[4] and of Friday Isaiah 11. 1–5.[5] Of the three Collects of Friday[6] the first, *Huius nobis parsimoniae* comes from *Leonianum,*[7] and is in the right place, as on the first Friday in Lent.[8] The second Collect, *Deus qui nostram,*[9] echoes the visitation theme of the Gospel of this day (Luke 1. 39–47): *aduentus tui uisitacione custodi.* The third, *Adesto, quaesumus,* may quite well have belonged originally to Wednesday and have been transferred hither.[10]

Wednesday.[11] The Introit of Wednesday is Psalm 18 (*Caeli enarrant*),[12] related to the coming of Christ, with the antiphon *Rorate caeli desuper* (Isaiah 45. 8), which is part of the fourth lesson of Saturday. The Offertory is *Aue Maria,* taken from the Gospel of this day, Luke 1. 28, from the Annunciation narrative. This also is a preparation for Christmas, as is the Communion *Ecce uirgo concipiet* (Isaiah 7. 14), which is drawn from the second lesson of this day.[13]

The two lessons of this day are Isaiah 2. 1–5, a Messianic prophecy about the Lord's house established on the top of the mountains and about beating swords into ploughshares, and Isaiah 7. 10–15, "Behold a Virgin shall conceive".[14] The Gospel of this day is the Annunciation, Luke 1. 26–38.[15] None of these propers has anything to do with Embertide: they are all of an Advent character, and can only date from the

[1] Gel. II, lxxxv, ed. Mohlberg, Nos. 1157–77.
[2] Gel. II, lx, ed. Mohlberg, Nos. 1037–52.
[3] Ed. Mohlberg, Nos. 1162, 1168, 1177.
[4] Würzburg, Nos. 161–2.
[5] Ibid., 163.
[6] Ed. Mohlberg, Nos. 1163–5.
[7] Ed. Feltoe, 169, 22; ed. Mohlberg, No. 1308.
[8] Gel. I, xviii, ed. Mohlberg, No. 124.
[9] Gel. II, lxxxv, ed Mohlberg, No. 1164.
[10] Chavasse, *Le sacramentaire gélasien,* pp. 410–12.
[11] I. Schuster, *The Sacramentary* (*Liber Sacramentorum*), London, 1924, I, pp. 329–33.
[12] Ed. Hesbert, No. 5.
[13] Frere, No. 143.
[14] Ibid.
[15] Frere, No. 269.

seventh century and later, when Advent was established in Roman liturgy.

Friday.[1] The Gradual of this day, *Benedixisti, Domine, terram tuam* (Ps. 84),[2] is about the coming of Christ. The Old Testament lesson concerns the sevenfold gifts of the Spirit (Isaiah 11. 1–5),[3] and the Gospel is the Visitation (Luke 1. 39–47).[4] This again is related to St John Baptist, an Advent theme, and to the coming of Christ.

Saturday.[5] The Gradual and the Communion of this day are from Psalm 18, as the Introit of Wednesday.[6] The six lessons before the Gospel are:[7]

Isaiah 19. 20–22.	A Saviour and defender against Egypt.
Isaiah 35. 1–7.	"The wilderness and the solitary place."
Isaiah 40. 9–11.	"O thou that tellest good tidings to Zion . . . He shall feed his flock."
Isaiah 45. 1–8.	"Drop down, ye heavens, from above."
Daniel 3.	The Three Holy Children.
2 Thess. 2. 1–8.	The Second Coming.

Except the Epistle, these are all concerned with the first coming of the Messiah, and are Advent in character, preparatory to Christmas. The Epistle speaks of the second Advent and in verse 8 it cites Isaiah 11. 4, which is part of Friday's lesson.

Everything cited so far is concerned with Advent and Christmas, and none of it with the fruits of the earth or with other thoughts of Embertide. Most of it is preserved in the Roman Missal of the present day. It represents an assimilation to Advent which was a product of the Gregorian reform, and has firmly established its place in Roman tradition ever since. But obviously this was not the theme before the invention of Advent. The original theme was much more closely connected with the usual background of Ember seasons.

Every one of the prayers of this Embertide in the Gregorian Sacramentary has reference to the coming of Christ.[8] The Leonine Sacramentary has agricultural references in the prayers of this week,[9] but references to the coming of Christ are already appearing in this book.[10] In the Gelasian Sacramentary the title is *Oraciones et praeces mensis decimi.*[11] This title must be older than the introduction of Advent: it is

[1] Schuster, op. cit., I, pp. 333–7. [2] Ed. Hesbert, No. 6.
[3] Frere, No. 144. [4] Frere, No. 270. [5] Schuster, op. cit., I, 337–51.
[6] Hesbert, No. 7. [7] Frere, No. 143. [8] Ed. Lietzmann, 189–91.
[9] E.g., ed. Mohlberg, Nos. 906, 910–13, 923, 1297, 1299.
[10] Ed. Mohlberg, Nos. 923–4, 1313. [11] Gel. II, lxxxv.

the ancient original title. The prayers [1] have hardly any reference to the Saviour's coming, but remain what they were in earlier times. The second collect of Wednesday has, however, been adapted to a position just before Christmas.[2] Originally it may not have belonged to this season: it occurs in the Gregorian in Lent,[3] as well as among *Orationes cottidianae*.[4] Its text there reads

te mereamur protegente saluari

but in the Gelasian *protegente* has been changed to *ueniente*. The second collect of Friday [5] has also a reference to the Advent:

aduentus tui uisitacione costodi

but this seems to be an addition, since this mass has three prayers before the Secret, which is one too many for Friday, which has only one lesson before the Gospel. The fifth collect of Saturday [6] modifies the original ending of a Gregorian collect used in Lent:[7] instead of

pro tua gloria misericorditer liberemur

it reads

pietatis tuae uisitacione consolemur.

This might be a reference to the Eucharistic action, and not to the Incarnation. The mass of Wednesday has two references to the Incarnation, in the Preface [8] and in the *Ad populum*,[9] which refers to the protection of Blessed Mary, the Gospel of this day being the Annunciation. Otherwise the themes of all these prayers are the usual Embertide subjects of prayer, fasting, and expulsion of demons, the last being referred to only in the *Ad populum* of Saturday.[10]

b. Lent. Practically the whole of the proper of these Ember Days is Lenten in character, and the traditional themes of Embertide are almost absent. The Ember liturgy has been even more thoroughly assimilated to its position in Lent than has the December Embertide to Advent, no doubt because Lent was organized long before Advent.[11]

So the chants are almost exclusively concerned with penitence.[12] The only exception to this concerning the chants is the four graduals of

[1] Ed. Mohlberg, Nos. 1157–77. [2] Ibid., 1158. [3] Pad. 208; Hadr. 53, 4.
[4] Hadr., 202, 4. [5] Ed. Mohlberg, No. 1164. [6] Ed. Mohlberg, No. 1173.
[7] Pad. 118, 167; Hadr. 32, 1; 44, 5. [8] Ed. Mohlberg, No. 1160.
[9] Ibid., 1162. [10] Ibid., 1177.
[11] See I. Schuster, op. cit., II, pp. 63–7, 70–8.
[12] Ed. Hesbert, Nos. 43, 45, 46.

Saturday[1] from Psalms 87, 102, 116, and 118; and some anthems on Wednesday and Friday from Psalm 24. There is no reference to the fruits of the earth.

The lessons similarly all have Lenten themes on Wednesday and Friday. On Wednesday we find Exodus 24. 12–18, the giving of the Law to Moses; and 3 Kings 19. 3–8, Elijah's forty-day fast.[2] On Friday the single lesson is Ezekiel 18. 20–8,[3] concerned with personal responsibility for sin. There is no reference on any of the three days to agriculture, but the spring fast does not coincide with any season of harvest, as do the other three more primitive Embertides. The lessons of Saturday are more closely related to Embertide. They certainly have connection with the Lenten fast, but they appear to have some relation to the ordinations.[4] The first, Deuteronomy 26. 15–19, is concerned with keeping God's commandments, and this appears to be a Lenten theme. The second, Deuteronomy 20. 22–5, is again about keeping the commandments and entering the Promised Land. The third (2 Maccabees 1. 23–7) is the sacrifice and prayer of the priests for Israel, i.e. for the Church; and the fourth (Ecclesiasticus 36. 1–10), a prayer for the conversion of heathen nations. The fifth is the usual Embertide lesson from Daniel 3; and the sixth is 1 Thessalonians 5. 14–23, containing general exhortations which would be quite suitable for ordinands. It is possible that this service was arranged by Gelasius, who was the first to appoint this day for ordinations. And it is to be noted that, although this mass is clearly a later addition in the Gelasian Sacramentary, the ordination services are placed on this Saturday, the first ordination day of the civil year and likewise of a Sacramentary which begins, as does *Gelasianum*, on Christmas Day.[5]

The Gospels of these days are on Wednesday, Matthew 12. 38–50,[6] the expulsion of evil spirits, an Embertide theme; on Friday, John 5. 1–15,[7] the healing at the Pool of Bethesda, a theme which is fitting to Ember Week and to Lent; and on Saturday, Matthew 17. 1–9,[8] the Transfiguration, which is related to the Passion and the Resurrection, and therefore suitable for Lent and not related to Embertide.

As to the prayers, nothing survives of the times when this Embertide was the fast of the first month and distinct from the first week of Lent, except the six prayers provided by the Gelasian for Saturday. The

[1] Ed. Hesbert, No. 46. [2] Ed. Frere, No. 29. [3] Ibid., No. 31. [4] Ibid., No. 32.

[5] A. G. Martimort, *L'église en prière*, pp. 744–5; C. Callewaert, "La semaine *mediana* dans l'ancien carême romain et les Quatre-Temps", in *R.B.*, 36 (1924), pp. 22 ff.; reprinted in *Sacris Erudiri* 1940, pp. 584–8.

[6] Ed. Frere, No. 64. [7] Ibid., No. 66. [8] Ibid., No. 67.

Gelasian makes no Embertide provision for the Wednesday or Friday: these days have Lenten collects and are ordinary ferias of Lent. Saturday has the title

ISTE ORATIONES QUAE SEQUUNTUR PRIMA SABBATO IN MENSE PRIMO SUNT DICENDAE

ORATIONES ET PRECES IN XII LECTIONES MENSE PRIMA [1]

Its six prayers [2] all refer to fasting, but do not seem to be specially Lenten. But they are clearly an addition to the Gelasian.[3] The first, *Deus qui delinquentes*,[4] comes from the Leonine;[5] the second,[6] *Omnium nostrorum*, from the Leonine also;[7] the third and fourth [8] are not in the Leonine or Gregorian or elsewhere in the Gelasian; but the fifth [9] is the *oratio super sindonem* of the third Wednesday in Lent in *Gelasianum*,[10] and the sixth, *Omnipotens sempiterne deus, qui per continentiam*,[11] is drawn from the second Friday in Lent,[12] and is also used on the first Monday in Lent [13] and on the fifth Saturday in Lent.[14]

c. Pentecost. The liturgy of the Pentecost Embertide [15] retains many of its original references to the fruits of the earth, and has later been assimilated to the octave of Pentecost and acquired texts referring to the Holy Spirit.

The chants in the Antiphonary refer principally to the Holy Spirit, and to the theme of praise.[16] They have been adapted to the later position of this fast in the week of Pentecost.

The lessons are more mixed in character. The two Old Testament lessons of Wednesday [17] are Wisdom 1. 1–7, concerned with wisdom and discipline, which are gifts of the Holy Spirit, and Isaiah 44. 1–3, concerning the Spirit. But on Friday [18] the lesson from Joel 2. 23–7 is about the fruits of harvest, an old lesson chosen for Embertide before the Octave of Pentecost was introduced. On Saturday there is a mixture of references to the fruits of the earth and to the Holy Spirit.[19] The first lesson, Joel 2. 28–32, is about the Divine Spirit; the second, Leviticus 23. 9–11, 15–17, 20, 21, speaks of the first-fruits of harvest, and the fifty days between the wave-offering and the meal-offering;

[1] Gel. I, xix. [2] Ed. Mohlberg, Nos. 134–9.
[3] A. Chavasse, *Le sacramentaire gélasien*, pp. 216 ff.
[4] Ed. Mohlberg, No. 134. [5] 109, 7, ed. Mohlberg, No. 861.
[6] Ed. Mohlberg, No. 135. [7] 111. 13, ed. Mohlberg, No. 878.
[8] Ed. Mohlberg, Nos. 136, 137. [9] Ibid., No. 138. [10] Ibid., No. 211.
[11] Ibid., No. 139. [12] Ibid., No. 184. [13] Ibid., No. 110. [14] Ibid., No. 278.
[15] See Schuster, op. cit., II, pp. 402–18. [16] Ed. Hesbert, Nos. 109–11.
[17] Ed. Frere, No. 97. [18] Ed. Frere, No. 98.
[19] Ed. Frere: not numbered, but following 98.

the third, Deuteronomy 26. 1–3, 7–11, is of the first-fruits, and the entry into the Promised Land; the fourth, Leviticus 26. 3–12, about the sabbatical year and the year of Jubilee; the fifth is the customary Daniel 3 lesson; and the last, the Epistle, is Romans 5. 1–5, of the love of God shed abroad in our hearts by the Holy Spirit. The last is the only one connected with Pentecost. The others were there before, and were retained when the week of Pentecost was organized at the end of the sixth century.

The Gospel of Wednesday in the early Roman Gospel Book was John 6. 44–51,[1] about the bread of life, and therefore with a reference to agriculture as well as to the Eucharist. But those of Friday [2] and Saturday,[3] Luke 5. 17–26, the cure of a paralytic, and Matthew 20. 29–34, the healing of two blind men, represent customary Ember themes of healing and expulsion of demons.[4]

The prayers of these days in the Leonine Sacramentary come from the time before the octave of Pentecost was introduced, and therefore are mainly concerned with the fast of the fourth month, under which title they appear in this Sacramentary, and not with the Holy Spirit, though in a few cases they refer to the feast of Pentecost, which has just been celebrated. Five of them have reference to enemies who are afflicting the Roman Church and people. These are:[5]

227. Praesta, Domine Deus noster, ut contra omnes fremitus impiorum mentis puritate uincamus, et qui nos in sua confidentes uirtute moliuntur affligere a nobis ieiunantibus subiugentur.

211. Da, quaesumus, ecclesiae tuae, misericors Deus, ut sancto Spiritu congregata hostili nullatenus incursione turbetur.

214. Adesto, Domine, quaesumus, populo tuo, et quem mysteriis caelestibus inbuisti ab hostium furore defende.

218. Exaudi, Domine, preces nostras, et sicut profanas mundi caligines sancti Spiritus luce euacuasti, sic hostes Romani nominis et inimicos catholicae professionis expugna.

219. Deus, qui uastatoris antiqui perfidiam uirtute filii tui et sancti Spiritus destruendo dedisti nobis de captiuitate uictoriam; concede, quaesumus, ut qui nos inpetere moliuntur potentiae tuae dextera conterantur.

Mgr Callewaert suggests [6] that all these collects, as well as the Preface

[1] Ed. Frere, No. 140. [2] Ibid., 141. [3] Ibid., 142.

[4] See also A. G. Martimort, *L'église en prière*, pp. 723 ff.

[5] Ed. Mohlberg, whose numbering is here followed.

[6] C. Callewaert, "S. Léon le Grand et les textes du Léonien", in *Sacris Erudiri*, I, Bruges, 1948, pp. 71–8.

Post illos laetitiae dies, which will be considered later, were composed by St Leo himself in 455, when the Vandals under Gaiseric were investing Rome. The collect *Praesta, Domine* is related to Leo's Sermon 78, which was preached on Whitsunday, 12 June 455, in preparation for the ensuing Ember fast. On that day Gaiseric was attacking Rome, and he took it on 15 June, Ember Wednesday, and occupied it until 29 June, taking away thousands of captives and pillaging all the basilicas except SS Peter and Paul and perhaps the Lateran. If the collect *Praesta, Domine* were composed for that day of Pentecost, its references to the *fremitus impiorum* would aptly fit the imminent threat of invasion by an Arian army; *moliuntur affligere* would suggest that the siege was being prepared but was not yet launched; and *a nobis ieiunantibus* would be an apposite reference to the impending fast. Collects 211, 214, and 218 refer to enemies, of whom 218 speaks as enemies of the Roman people and of the Catholic religion, and 219 refers to the attack designed against the city. The last two collects have a title, in each case drawn from the text of the prayer, which is an unusual feature in the Leonine Sacramentary. The title of 218 is CONTRA INIMICOS CATHOLICAE PROFESSIONIS, and of 219 CONTRA IMPETITORES. The *cursus* of these prayers is similar to that of St Leo, and there seems sufficient evidence to justify their attribution to his hand, and if so, to the Pentecost of 455.

The Preface of Wednesday sets forth the fast in its relation to the fifty days of Eastertide, and, if it is compared with Sermon 78 of St Leo, the language of the two is seen to be very closely connected.[1]

Sermo 78, iii	*Leonianum 229*
Igitur *post* sanctae *laetitiae dies quos in honorem Domini a mortuis resurgentis* ac deinde *in caelos ascendentis exegimus postque perceptum sancti Spiritus donum* salubriter et *necessarie* consuetudo est ordinata *ieiunii*; ut si quid forte inter ipsa festiuitatum gaudia negligens libertas et licentia inordinata praesumpsit, hoc religiosae abstinentiae censura castiget; quae ob hoc quoque studiosius exsequenda est, ut illa in nobis *quae* hac die *ecclesiae diuinitus sunt collata permaneant* . . .	Vere dignum . . . *post* illos enim *laetitiae dies quos in honorem Domini a mortuis resurgentis* et *in caelos ascendentis exigimus* (lege *exegimus*) *postque perceptum sancti Spiritus donum necessarie* nobis haec *ieiunia* sancta prouisa sunt, ut pura conuersatione uiuentibus *quae diuinitus ecclesiae sunt collata permaneant.*

[1] C. Callewaert, op. cit., pp. 40–1; *Leonianum*, ed. Feltoe, p. 28; ed. Mohlberg, No. 229; cf. *Gelasianum*, ed. Mohlberg, No. 658.

Callewaert believes that the sermon and the preface were composed by St Leo. It might be that the preface was copied from St Leo's sermon, by St Leo or by a later hand; or that in the sermon St Leo quoted verbally an existing liturgical text, or that both drew from a common source. The possibility that St Leo quoted an existing liturgical text is defended with impressive argument by Professor F. L. Cross,[1] who shows that it was a habit of St Leo to cite existing liturgical texts. In this case, which seems on the whole the most probable, the preface is earlier in date than St Leo's sermon of 455, and indeed, it may be noted that, unlike the five collects considered above, it has no reference to the imminent perils of invasion, but it does bring out the notion that the day of Pentecost (as yet without an octave) concludes the great fifty days of joy which extend from Easter. This concept was certainly approved by Leo, but is older than his time, and was in fact the usual way of looking at the matter until Pentecost acquired an octave later than the time of St Leo.

The provisions of the Gelasian Sacramentary, like those of the Leonine, assume that the great festal season of the fifty days is over, and that the Church then recurs to fasting. Accordingly, we find this preface *Post illos enim laetitiae dies* in the Gelasian.[2] There is no octave of Pentecost, and the provision for an octave Sunday in the Gelasian [3] is an addition made later to the original stratum which includes the *Orationes et preces mensis quarti*.[4] The masses contained in this last section, for the three Ember Days, are archaic in their structure. There are two collects on Wednesday, one on Friday, and six on Saturday. Wednesday and Friday have an *oratio super sindonem*, though Saturday lacks this prayer; but all three have an *Ad populum* at the end.[5] Wednesday and Saturday have proper prefaces;[6] that of Saturday is concerned purely with fasting, and does not occur in the Leonine; that of Wednesday is derived from the Leonine, and has just been considered.

In the Gregorian Sacramentary, however, the propers of these Ember Days have been thoroughly integrated into the octave of Pentecost, and their theme throughout is the Holy Spirit and his gifts.[7]

[1] F. L. Cross, "Pre-Leonine elements in the Proper of the Roman Mass", in *J.T.S.*, 50, Oxford, 1949, pp. 191–7.

[2] Ed. Mohlberg, No. 658. [3] Gel. I, lxxxiiii, ed. Mohlberg, Nos. 676–82.

[4] Gel. I, lxxxiii, ed. Mohlberg, Nos. 654–75.

[5] A. Chavasse, *Le sacramentaire gélasien*, p. 196.

[6] Ed. Mohlberg, Nos. 658 and 673.

[7] Ed. Lietzmann, Nos. 115–17; see A. Chavasse, *Le sacramentaire gélasien*, pp. 595–604.

d. September. This Embertide has the most fully preserved its ancient liturgical references to the crops and fruits, especially in the Old Testament lessons.[1] This is because, alone among the Embertides, it does not fall at any great season of the ecclesiastical year, and so has not absorbed their liturgical themes, as the Ember seasons have done in Advent, Lent, and Pentecost.

Its Old Testament lessons and texts refer to harvest, for example the Communion of Wednesday:[2]

> Comedite pinguia et bibite mustum

or to the seventh month, for example the Communion of Saturday:[3]

> Mense septimo festa celebrabitis cum in tabernaculis habitare fecerim filios Israhel cum educerem eos de terra Egypti ego Dominus Deus uester.

The Old Testament lessons of Wednesday [4] are Amos 9. 13–15, on abundance of fruits, and 2 Esdras 8. 1–10, which refers to the first day of the seventh month as a holy day. The lesson of Friday [5] is Hosea 14. 2–10, with agricultural references. On Saturday the Old Testament lessons [6] are from the Law and the Prophets, the first from Leviticus 23. 27–32, referring to the tenth day of the seventh month, a day of atonement and rest; and Leviticus 23. 39–43 is the second, about the fifteenth day of the seventh month, "the feast of tabernacles, when ye have gathered in the fruits", the third is Micah 7. 14, 16, 18–20, "Feed thy people with thy rod"; the fourth, Zechariah 8. 1, 2, 14–19, mentioning the fasts of the fourth, fifth, seventh, and tenth months as giving joy and gladness and cheerful feasts. The fifth lesson, as usual, is Daniel 3, and the Epistle is Hebrews 9. 2–12.

The Gospels are all concerned with healings, a standard Embertide theme. That of Wednesday (Mark 9. 17–29) is the healing of the deaf and dumb boy;[7] that of Friday (Luke 5. 17–26), the healing of a paralytic,[8] used also on the Friday in Pentecost;[9] that of Saturday,[10] the healing of a woman with a spirit of infirmity.[11]

The fifth prayer of Saturday is the customary *Deus qui tribus pueris*, following the Daniel lesson and related to it. The others in the Gelasian are concerned with the usual Ember themes.[12] They are principally

[1] Schuster, op. cit., III, pp. 150–67.
[2] Ed. Hesbert, No. 190.
[3] Ed. Hesbert, No. 192.
[4] Ed. Frere, No. 126.
[5] Ibid., No. 127.
[6] Ibid., No. 128.
[7] Ibid., No. 229.
[8] Ibid., No. 230.
[9] Ibid., No. 141.
[10] Ibid., No. 231.
[11] Luke 13. 10–17.
[12] Gel. II, lx, ed. Mohlberg, Nos. 1037–52.

concerned with fasting, but the Secret of Wednesday[1] speaks of fruits of the earth:

> Deus, qui de his terrae fructibus tua sacramenta constare uoluisti, praesta, quaesumus, ut opem nobis et praesentis uitae conferas et futurae.

The structure of these masses, however, is Gregorian and not Gelasian in type. There is no *super sindonem* on any of the three days; nor any *ad populum* on Wednesday and Friday, though there is on Saturday. Wednesday and Friday have two and one collects respectively, in accordance with the usual number of lessons. This Gregorian structure contrasts with the Gelasian structure of the Pentecost Ember Days in the Gelasian.

Conclusion

The origins of Ember Days are wrapped in obscurity, but it is certain that they were a Roman peculiarity, which only spread slowly to other parts of the Western Church, and likely that at first they were instituted to provide Roman Christians with a specific Christian devotion to draw away their attention from the pagan *feriae* of harvest. This accounts for their position in the year, at the seasons of the harvests of corn, wine, and oil in the Roman countryside in June, September, and December. For a long time, down to the Gelasian Sacramentary inclusive, they were spoken of as the fasts of the fourth, seventh, and tenth months, that is, in relation to the Roman civil year and not in relation to the ecclesiastical or liturgical year. These original three seasons were increased to four by the addition of a spring fast in March, which seems to have taken place about the middle of the sixth century.

The connection of three of the Embertides with the pagan *feriae* accounts for the frequent references to harvest which have survived in their liturgy down to the present day. Later they were used for ordinations, and a few of their propers seem to have been chosen with regard to this fact. There is some variation in the dates on which they were fixed, which persisted until the eleventh century. Originally

[1] Ed. Mohlberg, No. 1039.

they belonged to particular months of the civil year, a sign of their connection with a pagan background, and it is only about the time of the original *Gelasianum*, in the sixth century, that they began to be fixed in specific weeks of the ecclesiastical year, in the first week of Lent, in the week of Pentecost, and in the third week of Advent, the last full week before Christmas. This has never happened to the September fast, which is not fixed in a particular week after Pentecost, and therefore variable from year to year, but in the third week of September.

The liturgy of the Ember Days is among the most ancient survivals in the present Roman Missal, and has preserved many archaic features, which have disappeared from other parts of the year. There is practically no variation in all the ancient authorities respecting the station at St Peter on the Sunday before each Embertide (except on the first Sunday in Lent, which is of more ancient institution than the Embertide which follows it), or in regard to the stations of the three Ember Days, Wednesday at St Mary Major, Friday at the Holy Apostles, and Saturday at St Peter. With hardly any exceptions there are two Old Testament lessons before the Gospel on Wednesday, one on Friday, and five on Saturday, followed by an Epistle. The fifth lesson is from Daniel 3, followed by the Canticle *Benedictus es*.

There was an ancient tradition that ordinations of priests and deacons (as of bishops) must be ministered on Sunday, and later on ordinations were restricted to the Sundays after the Ember Weeks. The ordinations, however, were not on Sunday morning but during the night of Saturday to Sunday, at the Vigil mass, which is the Saturday mass of the Sacramentaries, Antiphonaries, and Lectionaries. This left Sunday vacant, and it had no mass of its own for a long time. Even when it was provided with a mass, as in the Gregorian Sacramentaries, it long retained its old title *Dominica uacat*.

The themes of the lessons are very mixed. Originally the same type of lessons seems to have served at all four fasts: lessons whose subject is prayer, fasting, the casting out of devils, healings, and fruits of the earth. These have been preserved in September, but the other Embertides, falling at a particular season of the ecclesiastical year, have been affected by the thoughts of that season; so that the December Embertide is full of Advent and Nativity themes, and has become a preparation for Christmas; the March Embertide is greatly affected by themes derived from Lent; and the June Embertide by meditations proper to the octave of the Holy Spirit.

III

What is *Mediana* Week?

What is Mediana *Week?*

1. THE TERM "MEDIANA"

Mediana is a term peculiar to Roman liturgy, and is applied to the fifth Sunday in Lent, to the Wednesday and Saturday which precede this Sunday, and to the week embracing these three days. The term first occurs in a letter of Pope Gelasius, written in 494,[1] in which he says that ordinations of priests and deacons should only be performed at certain seasons on Saturday evening, namely the fasts of the fourth, seventh, and tenth months, which are the original Embertides, on the first Saturday in Lent, which is in the fourth and later Embertide, and on the Saturday *medianae quadragesimae*. The term occurs again in the next century when Pope Pelagius I (556–61) appointed this *mediana septimana paschae* as a season for ordinations.[2] The text of Gelasius is quoted in the *Liber Diurnus*,[3] of which the earliest manuscript dates from the seventh or eighth century; in a letter of Gregory II in 715;[4] and in the eleventh canon of the Roman Council of 743.[5]

The term *mediana* Sunday is found in *Ordines Romani* XXVI, XXVII, XXVIII, XXIX, XXXI, L, xxi; which all state clearly that it was a Roman peculiarity:

> dominica quam sedis apostolica mediana uoluit nuncupari.

The title is found also in the Epistolary of Würzburg, a Roman book of the seventh century, and in the *Comes* of Murbach and the *Comes* of Alcuin in the eighth century. After this the term disappears from Roman liturgy, and it is not found in the Gelasian or Gregorian Sacramentaries.

2. CALLEWAERT'S THEORY

Mgr Callewaert explains these curious facts by saying that *mediana* is an extraordinary week, like the Ember Weeks, in that it is united with the following and not with the preceding Sunday. It shares its

[1] *Ep.*, 14 *ad uniuersos episcopos per Lucaniam*, 11, in Thiel, *Ep. Rom. Pontif.*, Braunsberg, 1868, I, pp. 368–9.

[2] P.L. 69, 416 D.

[3] P.L. 105, 75–6.

[4] P.L. 89, 502.

[5] Mansi, *Concilia*, XII, 384.

name with the Sunday which concludes it, instead of taking it from the Sunday which precedes it. *Mediana* week has certain other similarities with Ember Weeks, for instance in *Missale Romanum* it still preserves three lessons on Wednesday (two Prophetic and one Gospel), though it has lost one of the three on Saturday. *Flectamus genua* and *Leuate* have been preserved on the Wednesday, as on the Ember Days. Moreover at Rome between the fourth and the seventh centuries there were three weeks in Lent which had special solemnity, the first, which was Ember Week, the fourth, which was *mediana* week, and the sixth, which was Great Week. In these three weeks alone in Lent the *Comes* of Würzburg, which goes back to the early seventh century, provides more than two lessons. These weeks were weeks of more rigorous fasting than the others in Lent, and in the middle of the fifth century St Peter Chrysologus at Ravenna and St Maximus of Turin were aware of this, and disapproved of it. They wanted to establish a rigorous six-week fast, Sundays alone excepted.

3. CHAVASSE'S THEORY

Professor Chavasse rejects this explanation.[1] He thinks that the expression *mediana* is inexplicable in a Lent of forty days, and can only be explained in terms of a three-week Lent. The only evidence for the existence of a three-week Lent is provided by Socrates, the Greek ecclesiastical historian, writing about 439, who says that Rome has a continuous three-week fast before Easter, except for Saturdays and Sundays, by contrast with other Churches, which fasted for as much as seven weeks.

> οἱ μὲν γὰρ ἐν Ῥώμῃ τρεῖς πρὸ τοῦ Πάσχα ἑβδομάδας πλὴν Σαββάτου καὶ Κυριακῆς συνημμένας νηστεύουσιν.[2]

Rome certainly had a six-week fast before 385, and by that time it also fasted on Saturdays, which it had not done in earlier times. So Socrates is guilty of two errors in the one sentence. Chavasse accepts his evidence, and argues that in this three-week Lent, from our fourth Sunday until Easter Even, there were three Sundays, our fourth, fifth, and sixth; and that the middle Sunday of these three is the fifth, which is the one

[1] A. Chavasse, "La préparation de la Pâque, à Rome, avant le Ve siècle: Jeûne et organisation liturgique", in *Mémorial J. Chaine*, Lyon, 1950, pp. 61–80.

[2] *Hist. Eccl.* V, 22; P.G. 67, 632.

called *mediana* in these early Roman authorities; and the *mediana* week is then reckoned backwards from that Sunday, and begins on the Monday before, that is on the Monday after the fourth Sunday. It is reckoned backwards because you are counting back from Easter. This would seem to be more subtle than convincing. We may agree that the fifth Sunday in Lent is the middle Sunday of the last three before Easter, but on Chavasse's reckoning *mediana* week is the first of the last three if you count forward, and the last of the three if you count backward. The middle week of this period would be the one from the fifth to the sixth Sunday in Lent. And is it really true that the Roman Church reckoned backwards in this way, even if it is the case that the Roman tended to count time backwards for calendrical purposes from the Kalends, Nones, and Ides?

Moreover, this explanation depends entirely on the evidence of Socrates, which in this respect is untrustworthy. C. L. Feltoe says, "Socrates is notoriously ill-informed as to Roman matters, and his account here lacks verification in general, and in particular the omission of Saturdays from the fast is very un-Roman."[1] Long before the time of Socrates Rome fasted on Saturdays in Lent, and Lent was six weeks in length. Chavasse explains that Socrates is speaking of a period before his own time: the answer to this is that in that case he should not have used the present tense. As soon as Lent appears at all at Rome it has six weeks, forty days from the first Sunday (or sixth before Easter) to Maundy Thursday; and Good Friday and Easter Even are reckoned as part of the Paschal Solemnity, concluding on Easter Day, and are not really part of Lent.

4. CONCLUSION

I suggest therefore that Socrates may have misunderstood the distinctively Roman practice of Lent as a six-week disciplinary period, connected also with preparation for baptism, in which there were three weeks of special solemnity and more rigid fasting. In these weeks Saturday was a fast in the fourth century, which it was not at Rome in the other weeks of Lent until the fifth century. The three specially solemn weeks are not in fact συνημμέναι, as Socrates says, but discontinuous. One of these weeks is the first week in Lent, and is Ember

[1] C. L. Feltoe, "Aduersaria Liturgica", in *J.T.S.*, 2, Oxford, 1901; A. "Mediana Hebdomada Quadragesimae", pp. 130–7, esp. p. 133; cf. J. A. Jungmann, "Die Quadragesima in den Forschungen von A. Chavasse", in *Archiv für Liturgiewissenschaft*, 5 (1957), pp. 84–95.

Week, with ordinations on Saturday night; one is the last, which is Holy Week, with a Saturday Vigil at which baptism was administered; and the middle or *mediana* week of these three is the one which follows *media quadragesima*, i.e. the fourth Sunday, which is the twenty-second day of a forty-day Lent, near enough to the middle. It is quite possible that the fourth Sunday was, as *Laetare* Sunday was to be later in the Roman rite, a more joyful Sunday, which is a break half-way through Lent, and then immediately after it, on Monday, *mediana* week begins. Like the first week of Lent it is a specially solemn week, and like that week concludes with a Saturday vigil, at which Gelasius and Pelagius at least conferred holy orders. For this reason the fifth Sunday in Lent was, like the second Sunday, a *vacat* Sunday until the seventh century, with no proper liturgy, and it would have, like the Sundays after all Embertides, which long remained vacant, a connection with the week before rather than with the week following.

IV

The Offertory Prayers and the Canon of the Roman Mass

The Offertory Prayers and the Canon of the Roman Mass

The original offertory prayer of the Roman rite is the Secret, which commends the oblations to God and has always been a variable prayer, together with the Collect and the Post-communion. Fixed offertory prayers are a Gallican innovation, and this fact was known to Bernold of Constance, who speaks of *Veni sanctificator* as being *iuxta Gallicanum ordinem*, and of *Suscipe sancta Trinitas* as being a customary prayer, not derived from any *ordo*, and then says explicitly

> Romanus tamen ordo nullam orationem instituit post offerendam ante Secretam.[1]

The present offertory prayers of the Roman missal were first enjoined at Rome in the fourteenth century in *Ordo Romanus* XIV, 53, of Mabillon's enumeration,[2] and thence came into the 1570 Missal. They are of varying date, all older than the fourteenth century, and they present striking resemblances to the much older prayers of the Canon, which it is our purpose to set out in this essay.

SUSCIPE SANCTE PATER

This prayer first occurs in the prayer book of Charles the Bald (875–7).[3] It is rich in parallels to phrases in the Canon.

Offertory	*Canon*
Suscipe	*cf.* ut placatus *accipias* (HANC IGITUR).
sancte *Pater*	clementissime *Pater* (TE IGITUR)
hanc *immaculatam hostiam*	*hostiam immaculatam* (UNDE ET MEMORES)
quam ego indignus famulus tuus	quae *tibi offerimus* (TE IGITUR)
offero tibi	pro quibus *tibi offerimus* (MEMENTO DOMINE)
	offerimus praeclarae maiestati tuae (UNDE ET MEMORES)

[1] *Micrologus*, 11; P.L. 151, 984.

[2] P.L. 78, 1163–5.

[3] *Liber precationum quas Carolus Calvus Imp . . . colligi . . . mandavit*, ed. F. Felician, Ingolstadt, 1583, p. 112.

et pro *omnibus circumstantibus*	et *omnium circumstantium* (MEMENTO DOMINE)
pro omnibus *fidelibus christianis* uiuis atque defunctis	quorum tibi *fides* cognita est (MEMENTO DOMINE).
	qui nos praecesserunt cum signo *fidei*. (MEMENTO ETIAM.)
	cf. also in general the *Memento* of the living and of the dead.
ut mihi et illis proficiat *ad salutem*	pro spe *salutis* et incolumitatis suae. (MEMENTO DOMINE.)
	calicem *salutis* perpetuae (UNDE ET MEMORES).

DEUS QUI HUMANAE SUBSTANTIAE

This is by far the oldest of the offertory prayers, and was not written as such, but as a collect for Christmas in the Leonine Sacramentary.[1] It has been slightly altered to suit its present purpose. It draws nothing from the Canon.

OFFERIMUS TIBI

The prayer for the offering of the chalice is Mozarabic, and first occurs in the *Missale Mixtum*,[2] and is also found in several later missals and sacramentaries.

offerimus tibi, Domine, *calicem salutaris*.	*offerimus* praeclarae maiestati tuae . . . *calicem salutis perpetuae*. (UNDE ET MEMORES.)
in conspectu diuinae maiestatis tuae	*in conspectu diuinae maiestatis tuae* (SUPPLICES).
pro nostra et totius mundi *salute*.	*pro spe salutis* (MEMENTO DOMINE).

IN SPIRITU HUMILITATIS

This is based upon Daniel 3. 39–40. It is one of the more recent of the offertory prayers, but, like *Offerimus tibi*, it is of Mozarabic origin.[3]

in conspectu tuo	*in conspectu* diuinae maiestatis tuae (SUPPLICES).
ut *placeat* tibi	cf. ut *placatus* accipias. (HANC IGITUR.)

[1] *Sacramentarium Veronense*, No. 1239, ed. L. C. Mohlberg, *Rerum Ecclesiasticarum Documenta*. Series Maior. Fontes, I, Rome, 1956.

[2] P.L. 85, 536.

[3] P.L. 85, 112–13.

VENI SANCTIFICATOR

Bernold of Constance knew this, as we have seen, as a Gallican prayer.[1] It is a medieval modification of the Mozarabic form,[2] and is first found at Rome in *Ordo* VI, 10,[3] and it appears in the ninth century in the Stowe Missal.[4]

benedic hoc sacrificium	*benedicas* haec dona haec munera *haec* sancta *sacrificia* illibata. (TE IGITUR.)

SUSCIPE SANCTA TRINITAS

The fact that this prayer is addressed to the Holy Trinity at once betrays it as late, since it long remained the invariable rule at Rome that liturgical prayer is addressed only to the Father. It is in fact a Gallican prayer belonging to the diptychs, which in the Gallican rite were associated closely with the offertory. The names of the offerers were read at this point, and Decentius of Gubbio was evidently acquainted with this Gallican custom, in opposition to which Pope Innocent I in his letter of 416 maintained the Roman usage of citing the names of offerers within the Canon, *inter sacra mysteria.*[5] In Gaul the old Gallican usage of the diptychs was finally suppressed by Charlemagne in 789, and not long afterwards, in the ninth century, there begin to appear in the sacramentaries prayers beginning *Suscipe sancta Trinitas,* and commending the offerers and others. They appear to replace the diptychs. The present invariable Roman form was adopted from the thirteenth century onwards. It has many phrases drawn from the Canon, and it is especially noteworthy that in mentioning the great acts of redemption it lists the Passion, Resurrection, and Ascension of Christ, and excludes the Nativity. Mention of the Nativity had been not unknown in the Canon. Bernold of Constance knew and disapproved of it,[6] and it occurs in some medieval missals, of which the oldest to have it in the first hand is Reims 213, of the ninth century. It became more common in the tenth century, and was sometimes inserted by correctors into older missals.[7] The present offertory prayer *Suscipe sancta Trinitas* is in this respect closely parallel to the wording of the Canon and excludes the mention of the Nativity.

[1] *Micrologus,* 11; P.L. 151, 984.
[2] *Missale Mixtum*; P.L. 85, 113.
[3] P.L. 78, 993.
[4] Ed. G. F. Warner, *H.B.S.*, XXXII, p. 7.
[5] *Ep.*, 25, ii, 5; P.L. 20, 554.
[6] *Micrologus* 13; P.L. 151, 985.
[7] B. Botte, *Le canon de la messe romaine*, Louvain, 1935, p. 63.

hanc oblationem	*Hanc* igitur *oblationem.*
quam tibi offerimus *ob memoriam passionis resurrectionis et ascensionis* Iesu Christi *domini nostri*	Unde et *memores* Domine nos serui tui . . . eiusdem Filii tui *Domini nostri* tam beatae *Passionis*, necnon et ab inferis *resurrectionis* sed et in caelos gloriosae *ascensionis.*
beatae *Mariae semper Virginis*	gloriosae *semper Virginis Mariae.* (COMMUNICANTES) beata et gloriosa *semper Virgine* . . . *Maria.* (LIBERA NOS)
beati *Ioannis* Baptistae	cum *Ioanne* . . . (NOBIS QUOQUE)
sanctorum *Apostolorum Petri et Pauli*	beatorum *Apostolorum* ac Martyrum tuorum *Petri et Pauli.* (COMMUNICANTES) cum beatis *Apostolis* tuis *Petro et Paulo* (LIBERA NOS).
et omnium sanctorum	*et omnium sanctorum* tuorum (COMMUNICANTES) *et omnibus sanctis* tuis (NOBIS QUOQUE) *et omnibus sanctis* (LIBERA NOS)
quorum *memoriam* agimus	Communicantes et *memoriam* uenerantes

V

Cursus in the Roman Canon

Cursus in the Roman Canon

1. CURSUS IN EARLY ROMAN LITURGY

Anyone reading the Solemn Prayers of Good Friday in the Roman rite is at once struck by the clear distinction which exists between the biddings and the collects of this ancient intercession both in language and in rhythm, and closer examination shows that whereas the biddings are almost destitute of rhythmic endings, showing only four in the nine biddings (two each in Biddings VI and VII), the nine collects abound in them, and not one of them is without at least one. This enables us to conclude that the biddings are earlier than the collects.[1] For it is known that Roman liturgical composition, like the work of the papal chancery, conformed to the principles of the *cursus* from some time in the fourth century until the middle of the seventh. Presence of rhythmic endings is therefore useless for dating a document within this period, but in the case of writings before or after it, attention to the presence or absence of *cursus* can give a good indication of date. The *cursus* became the rule in the papal chancery from the time of Siricius (384–98), and disappeared after St Gregory the Great (604),[2] and in the case of liturgical composition it prevailed roughly from 350 or a little later till about 650. The collects of the three ancient Roman Sacramentaries abound in rhythmic endings. Dom Mocquereau collected about 1030 *clausulae* from the Leonine Sacramentary, of which only ten did not conform to the rules of the *cursus*.[3] The Gelasian and Gregorian Sacramentaries show a like adherence to this literary principle, and their prayers nearly all date from within the classic period of the *cursus*, from the fourth to the seventh centuries.

2. THE CANON

The Canon of the Mass contrasts sharply with the collects of the ancient sacramentaries in the paucity of rhythmic endings. Collects are often quite short, but sometimes have as many as three or even four

[1] See Essay I, pp. 45–7.
[2] E. Vacandard, art. "Cursus" in *D.A.C.L.*, III, 2, col. 3197.
[3] *Paléographie musicale*, IV, pp. 36 ff.

rhythmic *clausulae*. But in spite of its much greater length, the Canon, from *Te igitur* to the end of *Nobis quoque*, appears to have only twenty-two. Their distribution is somewhat uneven, and they occur most frequently in the parts of the Canon which we know to be later. We take the text of the Canon printed in Dom Bernard Botte's edition,[1] representing the earliest known recension of the Gregorian Canon, and we note in the right-hand column any differences between the two main textual families, the Hiberno-Gallican and the Roman, which affect any of the *clausulae* which we cite.

The endings are abbreviated as follows:

P = Planus. T = Tardus. V = Velox.
Tr = Trispondaicus.

The manuscripts of the Canon are cited as in Botte's edition:

B. Bobbio Missal.
F. *Missale Francorum.*
G. *Sangallensis* 348.
S. Stowe Missal.
Z. Zürich, Rheinau 30.

Te igitur

rogámus et pétimus	T	
régere dignéris	Tr	
órbe terrárum	P	orbem terrarum B (error)

Memento Domine

nóta deuótio	T	

Communicantes

sanctórum tuórum	P	
precibúsque concédas	P	
muniámur auxílio	T	

Hanc igitur

famíliae túae	P	
placátus accípias	T	placátus suscípias FS (also T)
páce dispónas	P	
damnatióne nos éripi	T	eripias FGSZ (not rhythmic)
grége numerári	Tr	

[1] B. Botte, *Le Canon de la messe romaine*, Louvain, 1935.

Quam oblationem

déus in ómnibus	T	
fácere dignéris	Tr	dignáre FS (also Tr)

Qui pridie

None.

Simili modo

None.

Unde et memores

plébs tua sáncta	P	
gloriósae ascensiónis	V	
salútis perpétuae	T	

Supra quae

respícere dignéris	Tr	aspícere dignéris BFS (also Tr)

Supplices te rogamus

grátia repleámur	V	grátia replémur S (Tr)

Memento etiam

indúlgeas deprecámur	V	

Nobis quoque peccatoribus

donáre dignéris	P	donáre dignáre S (also P)
largítor admítte	P	

The various parts of the Canon are known to be of differing ages, and this fact seems to be reflected in the literary style and in the rhythm. *Te igitur* was in existence by 416, the date of the letter of Innocent I to Decentius.[1] It has three *clausulae* which conform to the rules. The *Memento* of the living is at least as old, and shows one ending. *Communicantes*, with three, was in the mass before St Leo and probably by 416.[2]

Hanc igitur has five endings, and is the most rhythmic piece in the Canon. It was fixed part of the Canon from the time of St Gregory the Great, but before that date was restricted to certain feasts.[3] It is known that the words *diesque nostros* onwards were added by St Gregory to an existing formula, and they show no fewer than three endings.

[1] *Ep.* XXV. See B. Capelle, *Travaux liturgiques*, II, Louvain, 1962, pp. 245, 253–4.

[2] Ibid., pp. 254, 271–2.

[3] Ibid., pp. 254, 269.

Quam oblationem has two, but the Institution narrative, *Qui pridie* and *Simili modo*, appears to have none at all. This seems to point to its being the earliest part of the Canon.

Unde et memores has three endings, and *Supra quae* and *Supplices te rogamus* one each, as has *Memento etiam*, which was part of the Gregorian Canon at least from the time of St Gregory. *Nobis quoque* was added at some time in the fifth century, and has been attributed to Leo, Gelasius, and Symmachus. It has two rhythmic endings, both of which are *planus*, and this is St Leo's favourite ending, which may well point to him as the author.

The central part of the Canon, from *Quam oblationem* to the end of *Supplices te rogamus*, is known to have been in existence at the time when St Ambrose about 390 wrote the *De sacramentis*, in which it is quoted *in extenso*. In this part only seven of our twenty-two endings occur, and this is what we should expect, as it was probably composed before the *cursus* became prevalent. But its form in the Gregorian recension is by no means identical with that in *De sacramentis*. If we examine that part of the Canon which is quoted by St Ambrose, we discover that with one exception the phrases which have been cited above as rhythmic do not occur.[1] Instead of

> quam oblationem tu deus in omnibus quaesumus benedictam adscriptam ratam rationabilem acceptabilemque facere digneris

we have

> fac nobis oblationem adscriptam ratam rationabilem acceptabilem.

In *Unde et memores* the words *plebs tua sancta* do not occur in Ambrose's version; and instead of *salutis perpetuae*, which scans, he reads *uitae aeternae*, which does not. In place of the later *in caelos gloriosae ascensionis* he has *in caelum ascensionis*, which is also a *velox* ending, and which is the only rhythmic ending to occur in Ambrose's citation of the Canon. In *Supra quae* Ambrose does not read *respicere digneris et accepta habere*, but *ut hanc oblationem suscipias*, and the conclusion of *Supplices te rogamus* is not present in Ambrose.

Thus, with the exception of *gloriosae ascensionis*, which occurs in Ambrose in a different form, though still rhythmic, none of the seven *clausulae* in this central part of the Canon occurs in *De sacramentis* at all. Evidently these endings, like nearly all the others in the rest of the

[1] *De sacramentis*, IV, 5, 21; 6, 26; ed. O. Faller, C.S.E.L., LXXIII, 55, 57, Vienna, 1955.

Canon, are later modifications, stylistic if not substantial, and the Roman Canon, as received by St Ambrose some time before 390, must have shown only the slightest traces of *cursus* in its language. Had the Canon been a very recent composition when Ambrose received it at Milan, it would have been likely to show far more observance of the *cursus* rules, and the fact that it shows so little influence suggests that it must date from some time earlier than 390, and probably from the period 350–70.

VI

The Connection of the Prayers of the Roman Canon

The Connection of the Prayers of the Roman Canon

Since 1474 the Roman Canon has been printed in paragraphs, marked with initial letters, and divided by rubrics. The prayers *Communicantes, Hanc igitur oblationem, Supplices te rogamus, Memento etiam* and *Nobis quoque peccatoribus* have a conclusion, *Per* (*eundem*) *Christum Dominum nostrum*; and to this is added *Amen* in every case except the last.[1] The Canon therefore looks like a sequence of separate prayers or units. But originally, like other *anaphorae*, it must have been one continuous prayer with one full conclusion. The *Amen* after this is the people's solemn response to the great Eucharistic Prayer.

The present text of the Canon has been fairly uniform since about 700, but we have insufficient evidence to be able to say what its precise forms were between 350–70, when it seems to have come into existence, and 700. In this connection it may be worth while to study the methods by which, in the present text of the Canon, each section is linked to the next. Even though changes have been made in the early period in both the text of the prayers and in their order, as seems likely, the connections between the various parts must have received the attention of those who made the changes.

A preliminary question, however, must be, "Where does the Canon begin and end?"[2] Edmund Bishop, in his critical edition,[3] began at *Te igitur* and ended with the embolism to the Lord's Prayer, *Libera nos*. Dom Bernard Botte, in his edition,[4] began with *per omnia saecula saeculorum. Amen* at the end of the Secret, and concluded with *Pax Domini* and its response, after the embolism to the *Pater*. Dom Leo Eizenhöfer[5] began with *Dominus uobiscum* before *Sursum corda* and

[1] See F. Cabrol, "Canon romain", in *D.A.C.L.*, II, 1899–1900; P. Salmon, "Les 'Amen' du canon de la messe", in *E.L.*, 42, Rome, 1928, pp. 496–506; G. Ellard, "Interpolated Amens in the Canon of the Mass", in *Theological Studies*, VI, U.S.A., 1945, pp. 380–91.

[2] See F. Cabrol, "Canon romain", in *D.A.C.L.*, II, 1848 ff.

[3] *Liturgica Historica*, Oxford, 1918, pp. 83–91.

[4] *Le canon de la messe romaine*, Louvain, 1935.

[5] *Canon missae romanae*, Rome, 1954.

ended with *Pax Domini* and the response. It is, however, generally agreed that the Canon ends with the conclusion, and before the *Pater* and the Fraction. The Canon is the Eucharistic Prayer, containing the consecration, and it stands apart from the other three actions which are set forth in the mass; from the offertory, which is placed before it; and from the fraction and the communion, which follow it. This suggests that the Canon begins at *Dominus uobiscum* before the Preface, since that follows the Secret, which is an offertory prayer and commends the gifts to God; and that it ends with the conclusion and *Amen*, which are then followed by the Lord's Prayer with its introduction and embolism. This last suggestion is in accord with the words of St Gregory the Great, who says that he placed the Lord's Prayer (in its present position) *mox post precem*, i.e. immediately after the end of the *prex* or Canon.[1]

There has been much more division of opinion concerning the beginning of the Canon. In printed missals it clearly begins at *Te igitur*. Between the eighth and tenth centuries the T of *Te igitur* was illuminated, and became a picture of the crucifix, and after the twelfth century this picture tended to be separated from the text and to become a plate on the page before *Te igitur* and the rest of the Canon. It has become customary to insert a large heading CANON MISSAE above *Te igitur*, and the Canon from that point is often printed in 48-point type which the printers call "Canon".[2] Yet in the Gelasian Sacramentary (*Vaticanus Reginensis* 316) of the eighth century, *Te igitur* does not even start a new line. In this book the Canon begins at *Sursum corda*, which begins section xvii of Book III, under a title INCIPIT CANON ACCIONIS,[3] and this is also the case in the *Missale Francorum*.[4] The theory that the Canon begins at *Te igitur* was without doubt greatly helped by the distinction which has existed for many centuries between the vocal Preface, sung or said in an audible voice, and the Canon, recited silently. But this distinction is not primitive, and did not arise until in the eighth

[1] S. Greg., *Registrum*, 9, 25, ed. Ewald-Hartmann, II, pp. 59–60: Orationem uero dominicam idcirco mox post precem dicimus. . . . Cf. Bernold of Constance, *Micrologus* X; P.L. CLI, 983; and see C. Lambot, "Le Pater dans la liturgie apostolique d'après s. Grégoire", in *R.B.*, 42 (1930), pp. 265–9.

[2] J. A. Jungmann, *The Mass of the Roman Rite*, London, 1961, pp. 365–6.

[3] Ed. Mohlberg, *Rerum Ecclesiasticarum Documenta*, Series Maior, Fontes, IV, *Liber Sacramentorum Romanae Aeclesiae Ordinis Anni Circuli* (*Sacramentarium Gelasianum*), Rome, 1960, No. 1242.

[4] Ed. Mohlberg, *Rerum Ecclesiasticarum Documenta*, Series Maior, Fontes, II, *Missale Francorum*, Rome, 1957, sec. 23, No. 156.

century the Canon came to be said silently, which was not the case in the formative centuries.

I. TE IGITUR

If *Te igitur* is indeed the beginning of the Canon, the connecting word raises a grave problem. *Igitur*, "therefore", must refer to something which precedes. And if nothing precedes, but if this is the beginning of the great prayer, *igitur* is left hanging in the air. Attempts have been made to explain this by postulating a different position for the prayer *Te igitur*, and it is indeed quite possible that originally it was somewhere else. It is not quoted in *De sacramentis*, where the Canon citation begins

Fac nobis hanc oblationem adscriptam, ratam . . .

But it has evidently been in this position at least since 416, the date of the letter of Innocent I to Decentius of Gubbio. Some authorities, feeling the difficulty of beginning a solemn prayer with a connective referring to something which precedes, have attempted to solve it by diminishing the force of *igitur*. Thus we are assured by Professor N. M. Denis-Boulet that "*igitur* n'a guère qu'une valeur explétive";[1] and Dom Bernard Botte and Professor Christine Mohrmann do not express *igitur* in their French translation, and comment that in fourth-century Latin *igitur* is no stronger than the Greek δέ.[2] But it must still mean something, and what can it mean if it begins the Canon? Dr Paul Drews thought that originally this prayer came, with other intercessory prayers, after the Consecration, as in the Liturgy of St James.[3] If this were so, *igitur* would refer to the consecration, and we should ask God to accept the consecrated gifts because of Christ's action at the Last Supper.

Even if *Te igitur* were originally in some other place, those who moved it to its present place, probably at the beginning of the fifth century, between *De sacramentis* in 390 and the letter of Innocent I in 416, must have intended *igitur* to mean something, or they would have removed it. There is no hesitation in the manuscript tradition: no single manuscript omits *igitur* or substitutes anything else. Can it be

[1] In A. G. Martimort, *L'eglise en prière*, Tournai, 1961, p. 392.

[2] *L'ordinaire de la messe*, Paris and Louvain, 1953, p. 75.

[3] See A. Fortescue, *The Mass: A Study of the Roman Liturgy*, London, 1937, pp. 156–60.

explained in its present position? It follows the Preface and, as we have seen, down to the eighth century at least, the *Sursum corda* and Preface were regarded as beginning the Canon. The *Sanctus* is not as early as the Preface.[1] There is no *Sanctus* in the Eucharistic Prayer of Hippolytus in the *Apostolic Tradition*. By the time of Serapion about 350, and in the liturgy of the eighth book of the Apostolic Constitutions, it has appeared, but it was evidently not used at every mass, since two hundred years later the Council of Vaison of 5 November 529 extended its use from public to private masses.[2] It is first mentioned in Africa in 484 by Victor Vitensis,[3] and at Rome the earliest evidence of it is of the sixth century.[4]

If there is no *Sanctus* the connection between the Preface and *Te igitur* is indeed very close. Professor Ratcliff well expresses this:

> If it be remembered that, as in the Eastern Liturgies, so in the Roman, the *Sanctus* is an interpolation, *Te igitur* will be seen to carry on the thought of the Preface. The sequence is *Vere dignum et iustum est . . . tibi gratias agere—Te igitur . . . supplices rogamus . . . uti accepta habeas . . . haec dona*. The sacrifice is here conceived in accordance with the Irenaean tradition.[5]

The sacrifice offered is described shortly afterwards, in the *Memento* of the Living, as *hoc sacrificium laudis*, so that it gives very good sense to connect the duty of thanksgiving with the sacrifice of praise, and the sequence

> It is very meet . . . that we should give thanks to thee . . . we therefore humbly beseech thee . . . to accept and bless these gifts . . . which we offer to thee for thy holy Catholic Church . . . Remember, O Lord, thy servants and handmaidens, and all who stand around . . . who offer to thee this sacrifice of praise for themselves and all theirs. . . .

is entirely natural.

[1] L. Chavoutier, "Un libellus pseudo-ambrosien sur le Saint-Esprit", in *Sacris Erudiri*, 11, Bruges, 1960, pp. 136–92.

[2] Canon 3, ap. G. Morin, *S. Caesarii Episcopi Arelatensis Opera Omnia*, II, 87, Maretioli, 1942: Et in omnibus missis seu in matutinis seu in quadragesimalibus seu in illis quae pro defunctorum commemoratione fiunt, semper *Sanctus, sanctus, sanctus* eo ordine quomodo ad missas publicas dicitur dici debeat. . . .

[3] *Historia persecutionis Africanae prouinciae*, C.S.E.L., VII, 70–1.

[4] *Liber Pontificalis*, ed. Duchesne, I, p. 128.

[5] "Christian Worship and Liturgy", in K. E. Kirk, *The Study of Theology*, London, 1939, p. 443.

2. MEMENTO

The Commemoration of the Living [1] has no connection with the end of *Te igitur* but begins:

> Memento domine famulorum famularumque tuarum et omnium circum adstantium.

The Stowe Missal begins *Memento etiam*, but there is no other variant in the manuscripts. Although *Memento* has thus no grammatical connection with *Te igitur*, it follows it naturally if the content of both prayers is considered. *Te igitur* commends the oblations and intercedes for the Church and in particular for the bishops.[2] We then go on to intercede for the living, and especially for those present, that is the offerers and communicants. The commendation of the offerings and intercession for the offerers fit well together. It appears from the letter of Innocent I to Decentius that *Te igitur* and *Memento* were together by 416:

> Prius ergo oblationes sunt commendandae ac tunc eorum nomina quorum sunt edicenda.[3]

but before that it seems probable that the Commemoration of the Living and of the Departed, which together form the diptychs, were read together at the Offertory. They have retained that position in most liturgies, though not in the Roman rite, and they were read by the deacon and not by the celebrant, as they are at present in the Roman rite.[4] When the Canon came to be said silently, it ceased to be possible for the deacon to read the list aloud.

If the lists of living and dead were at one time read together, the addition to *etiam* to *Memento* in the Commemoration of the Dead would be more easily explicable than it is in its present position.

3. COMMUNICANTES

Communicantes [5] is the only participle which occurs in the whole

[1] See F. Cabrol, in *Paléographie musicale*, V, Solesmes, 1896, pp. 71–8.

[2] See B. Capelle, "Et omnibus orthodoxis atque apostolicae fidei cultoribus" in *Miscellanea historica A. de Meyer*, Louvain, 1946, pp. 137–50, reprinted in B. Capelle, *Travaux liturgiques*, II, pp. 258–68, Louvain, 1962.

[3] Innocent, *Ep.* XXV, ii, 5; P.L. 20, 554.

[4] See F. Cabrol, *D.A.C.L.*, II, 1902.

[5] See C. Callewaert, "S. Léon, le 'Communicantes' et le 'Nobis quoque peccatoribus'", in *Sacris Erudiri*, I, Bruges, 1948, pp. 123–64.

Canon as a connective between two paragraphs. It links the prayer which follows with the *Memento* of the Living, and its antecedent is

> famulorum famularumque tuarum et omnium circum adstantium . . . qui tibi offerunt . . . tibi reddunt uota sua. . . .

The main difficulty in understanding it is not in relation to what precedes but to what follows. *Communicantes* ought naturally to be followed by *cum*: "communicating with" somebody, sharing in fellowship or communion with them. But nothing is dependent on it, and it is followed by *memoriam uenerantes* followed by a list of saints in the genitive. *Communicantes et memoriam uenerantes* will have to be taken as a hendiadys, the subsequent nouns in the genitive being dependent upon *memoriam uenerantes*, which is nearer to them.[1] The difficulty about this is that on the feasts of Christmas, Epiphany, Maundy Thursday, Easter Day, Ascension Day, and Pentecost, when there is a proper *Communicantes*, a phrase is inserted immediately after that word and before *memoriam uenerantes*. But these variable *Communicantes* do not go back earlier than the middle of the fifth century, and the simple ferial form of *Communicantes* was in existence before that time. Cardinal Schuster suggests that the participle originally followed the *Te igitur* in the form,

> cum beatissimo famulo tuo papa nostro illo communicantes

"communicating with thy blessed servant our bishop N.", *Memento* having been inserted later. Dom Bernard Botte suggests that *Communicantes* has an absolute sense, and stands independently, meaning "being in communion (with the Catholic Church)";[2] Dom Capelle, that the phrase means "communiant aux saints par la mémoire que nous en faisons";[3] Father Jungmann notes the absence of *-que* in the ancient form of *tibique reddunt uota sua*. *-que* is omitted by all early manuscripts: its first appearance is in *Padua D* 47.[4] Jungmann accordingly suggests that a full-stop should be placed after *incolumitatis suae*, and a fresh beginning made with

> Tibi reddunt uota sua aeterno deo uiuo et uero communicantes.[5]

[1] This view is held by Dom B. Capelle, "Problèmes du 'Communicantes' de la messe", in *Travaux liturgiques*, II, pp. 271–2; and by Dom B. Botte, *Le canon de la messe romaine*, p. 56.

[2] *Le Canon de la messe romaine*, Louvain, 1935, pp. 55–6.

[3] *Travaux liturgiques*, II, 272.

[4] See apparatus in Botte, op. cit., p. 34.

[5] J. A. Jungmann, *The Mass of the Roman Rite*, London, 1961, p. 401.

This is certainly smoother than the punctuation and division of the present missal, but it does not solve the problem of the meaning of the participle *Communicantes*.

Being a participle, it must be knit, unless it is substantival, to something which precedes, but it is not connected with what follows, *Hanc igitur*, because at an early date a conclusion, *per christum dominum nostrum* has been inserted, to which *amen* was added by the 1474 Missal. *Communicantes* has, however, closer relations with the two prayers which precede than with those which follow, *Hanc igitur* and *Quam oblationem*. With *Te igitur* and *Memento* it certainly forms part of the intercession of the Roman Canon, which the following prayers do not.

4. HANC IGITUR OBLATIONEM

Igitur occurs twice in the Canon as a connecting word, here and in *Te igitur*. In both cases the prayer asks God to accept the gifts because of something which has preceded. In the former case because it is very meet and right that we should give thanks, we ask God *therefore* to accept and bless our gifts:

> Te igitur . . . supplices rogamus et petimus uti accepta habeas et benedicas haec dona haec munera haec sancta sacrificia inlibata.

In this case because we have commemorated the offerers (*Memento*) and because of the fact that we offer in fellowship with and in pious commemoration of the saints (*Communicantes et memoriam uenerantes*) we *therefore* ask God to accept our oblation:

> Hanc igitur oblationem seruitutis nostrae sed et cunctae familiae tuae quaesumus domine ut placatus accipias.

It is well known, from the *Liber Pontificalis*,[1] from the Venerable Bede,[2] and from John the Deacon,[3] that the second part of *Hanc igitur*, from *diesque nostros*, was added by St Gregory the Great, and in the Leonine Sacramentary, dating from the century before St Gregory, it does not appear. The prayer was for a long time variable. There are ten variants in the Leonine Sacramentary, and forty-one in the old Gelasian, but only six in the Gregorian, which have now been reduced to three in *Missale Romanum*. It was not fixed in its present form before the ninth

[1] Ed. Duchesne, I, p. 312.

[2] *Hist. Eccles. Gentis Anglorum*, II, 1, ed. C. Plummer, Oxford, 1896, I, p. 78; P.L. 95, 80.

[3] *Greg. Magni Vita*, II, 17; P.L. 75, 94.

or tenth century, but the Leonine Sacramentary shows that its purpose was to express the general intention of the offerers, and this is why it is grammatically connected with the *Memento* and the *Communicantes*.[1]

5. QUAM OBLATIONEM

The Canon as cited by St Ambrose begins at this point, and he quotes no prayers before it, though he refers to praises and to intercessions, but begins absolutely:

> Fac nobis hanc oblationem adscriptam rationabilem acceptabilem quod est figura corporis et sanguinis domini nostri Iesu Christi qui pridie quam pateretur . . . [2]

Ambrose's eucharistic prayer is a continuous whole, uninterrupted by conclusions or *Amens*.

If in the fourth century this was the original beginning of the Roman eucharistic prayer, it has been adjusted to fit in with the intercessory prayers which now precede, and the connection of a relative is close, and binds the prayer to the words *Hanc igitur oblationem* which begin the previous prayer. It thus refers to the same oblation, and prays for its acceptance in more explicit terms than *Hanc igitur*, which simply asks that the oblation may be accepted. *Quam oblationem* asks that God would make it

> benedictam adscriptam ratam rationabilem acceptabilemque

(in which *benedictam* and *ratam* have been added to the form existing in the time of Ambrose) and this in order that it may become to us the Body and Blood of Christ.

6. QUI PRIDIE

The recital of the institution is the core of all eucharistic prayers, and in every anaphora it is united to whatever precedes by the relative pronoun. This is a striking fact. For the narrative of the institution is derived directly from scripture, though it is usually a conflate text, and not drawn purely from any one of the institution narratives in the Gospels. It draws elements from them, and from the account in

[1] See B. Botte, *Le canon de la messe romaine*, Louvain, 1935, pp. 58–9; J. A. Jungmann, *The Mass of the Roman Rite*, London, 1961, pp. 409–13; V. L. Kennedy, "The pre-Gregorian 'Hanc igitur'" in *E.L.*, 1936, pp. 349–58.

[2] *De sacramentis*, IV, 5, 21, ed. O. Faller, C.S.E.L., 73, p. 55, Vienna, 1955.

1 Corinthians, and from the Feeding of the Multitude, and in the Roman Canon is still further expanded by such phrases as

in sanctas ac uenerabiles manus suas
hunc praeclarum calicem in sanctas ac uenerabiles manus suas
et aeterni
mysterium fidei.

Subject, however, to the addition of such elaborations, the institution narrative consists mainly of the dominical words from scripture, and is thus different from the prayers of the Canon which precede it.[1] It is therefore all the more remarkable that it should be cast in the form of a relative clause closely depending upon what precedes. The antecedent of *Qui* is the genitive *dilectissimi filii tui domini dei nostri Iesu Christi* at the end of *Quam oblationem*. The consecration of the chalice is united to that of the bread by the opening *Simili modo* (in Ambrose and tbe *Apostolic Tradition Similiter etiam*). Thus the institution narrative is firmly embedded in a continuous action proceeding from the thanksgiving of the Preface through the intercession and the prayers for acceptance of the gifts to the consecration of the gifts.

7. UNDE ET MEMORES

The flow of the prayer is continued in the Anamnesis: "Wherefore we remembering . . . thy Son's . . . passion . . . resurrection . . . and ascension offer . . . ". St Ambrose's citation is not quite the same in wording, but the variants are not significant. He reads

Ergo memores gloriosissimae eius passionis et ab inferis resurrectionis et in caelum ascensionis offerimus tibi hanc immaculatam hostiam rationabilem hostiam incruentam hostiam hunc panem sanctum et calicem uitae aeternae.[2]

Unde, "wherefore", refers to the institution narrative. It is because our Lord performed these acts at the Supper, and commanded us to continue to perform them for a memorial of him, that we, having in mind his Passion, Resurrection, and Ascension, make this pure and holy offering.

[1] See E. C. Ratcliff, "The Institution Narrative of the Roman *Canon Missae*: Its beginnings and early background", in *Studia Patristica*, II, pp. 64–82, *Texte und Untersuchungen*, LXIV, Berlin, 1957.

[2] *De sacramentis*, IV, 6, 27, ed. O. Faller, C.S.E.L., 73, Vienna, 1955, p. 57.

8. SUPRA QUAE

The Canon cited by St Ambrose has a prayer after the Anamnesis, beginning

Et petimus et precamur uti hanc oblationem suscipias in sublime altare tuum.[1]

which combines the petitions of the present *Supra quae* and *Supplices te rogamus*. The form quoted in *De sacramentis* no doubt represents an earlier stage of the Roman Canon. In the present rearrangement the petition for the acceptance by God of the offering is more closely knit to *Unde et memores* by the relative *quae* at the beginning, which unites it as closely as possible to what has gone before.[2] The antecedent of *quae* is the

panem sanctum uitae aeternae et calicem salutis perpetuae

which come at the end of *Unde et memores*. In that prayer we offered these holy gifts, now consecrated, and now we ask God graciously to look upon them and to accept them, as he accepted the offerings of Abel, Abraham, and Melchisedech in the Old Testament.

9. SUPPLICES TE ROGAMUS

If we set aside the *Memento* of the Living, which, with that of the Departed, may have been an insertion into the original Canon, *Supplices* is the only part of the Canon not joined to what precedes by either a relative or a conjunction. It does, however, say

iube haec perferri . . . in sublime altare tuum

in which phrase *haec* refers back through *quae* of *Supra quae* to the consecrated gifts, the *panem sanctum uitae aeternae et calicem salutis perpetuae* of *Unde et memores*. This prayer is, however, a composition of the sixth century, and is not original. Dom Bernard Botte remarks that its wording is divisible into three parts, of which *supplices te rogamus, omnipotens deus* is derived from a post-communion in the Gregorian, and is not paralleled exactly in the earlier sacramentaries; *iube haec perferri . . . maiestatis tuae* has a parallel in the *De sacramentis*,[3] and is therefore of the fourth century; and the rest is the end of an epiclesis.[4]

[1] *De Sacr*, IV, 6, 27, C.S.E.L. 73, p. 57.
[2] See C. Mohrmann, "Quelques observations sur l'évolution stylistique du canon de la messe romaine", in *Vigiliae Christianae*, 4, Amsterdam, 1950, p. 8.
[3] *De sacr.*, IV, 6, 27, ed. O. Faller, C.S.E.L., 73, Vienna, 1955, p. 57: uti hanc oblationem suscipias in sublime altare tuum per manus angelorum tuorum.
[4] B. Botte, *Le canon de la messe romaine*, Louvain, 1935, p. 66.

Had it been original, its connection might have been closer, and indeed in Ambrose it appears in a very different form, and the fact that it was added in its present form at a later date is betrayed by the presence of a conclusion, *per Christum dominum nostrum*.

10. MEMENTO ETIAM

This is an opening which does not connect at all naturally with the ending of the previous section, with or without *per Christum dominum nostrum*. But it would connect very well with the *Memento* of the Living,[1] for then we should have

> Memento domine famulorum famularumque tuarum et omnium circum adstantium . . . qui tibi offerunt hoc sacrificium laudis . . .
>
> Memento etiam domine famulorum famularumque tuarum . . . qui nos praecesserunt cum signo fidei et dormiunt in somno pacis . . .

The parallelism would be striking, and if these pieces originated as the two parallel prayers of the diptychs of living and departed at the Offertory, it would be easy to see their balance. Dom F. Cabrol held the view that this was their original position,[2] and Edmund Bishop agreed.[3] The difficulty of this view is that it makes it hard to explain why *etiam* was not changed when the commemoration of the departed was inserted at this point, and in any case why it was separated from the commemoration of the living, and placed after the consecration and not with the commemoration of the living before the consecration. A possible explanation of this separation is that it was desired to place the commemoration of the faithful departed immediately before the commemoration of the saints with which the Canon ends, namely *Nobis quoque peccatoribus*. This comes naturally enough at the end, and a position immediately before it is a suitable one for the faithful departed. There is, however, a further difficulty in that the *Memento* of the Departed is not in the Ambrosian Canon in *De sacramentis*, nor did it become a fixed part of the canon till as late as the ninth century. It was used on weekdays, but not on Sundays, and is not to be found in canons intended for Sunday or solemn stational use. Thus it does not appear in *Vaticanus Reginensis lat* 337 (ninth century) nor in Cambrai 164 (159), nor in the old Gelasian (*Vaticanus Reginensis* 316); all of

[1] F. Cabrol, in *Paléographie musicale*, V, Solesmes, 1896, pp. 78–81.
[2] *D.A.C.L.*, II, 1903.
[3] *Liturgica Historica*, Oxford, 1918, pp. 96–103, 109–15.

them Gregorian in the Canon, and representing authentic Roman usage. Yet its language is thoroughly archaic, and it must have existed, even if not part of the Canon, earlier than the sixth century.[1]

11. NOBIS QUOQUE PECCATORIBUS

This opening cannot refer back to *Supplices te rogamus*, as "we sinners" (*nobis peccatoribus*) and "as many as shall receive the Body and Blood" (*quotquot ex hac altaris participatione sacrosanctum filii tui corpus et sanguinem sumpserimus*) refer to the same people, the communicants. Unless, therefore, it refers to some clause which has disappeared, it must refer to the *Memento* of the Departed.[2] It would do this naturally enough, "Remember thy servants who have departed with the sign of faith . . . and to us also thy sinful servants . . . grant some share and fellowship with thy holy Apostles . . . ", but it appears that *Nobis quoque* was in the Canon long before the *Memento* of the Departed was a regular daily part of the Canon; and indeed *Nobis quoque* is included by the Gelasian and Gregorian manuscripts which omit the *Memento* of the Dead. If so, *quoque* would not have been a good connective except on those days when the *Memento* of the Departed was used. Was there a time when the word *quoque* was absent? There is no sign of this in Dom Botte's apparatus, and indeed Botte describes *Nobis quoque* as a sort of embolism to *Memento etiam*.[3] Father Jungmann makes a suggestion which would solve this difficulty, namely that *Nobis quoque peccatoribus* refers to the clergy and not to the Church in general, and therefore is not in fact referring to the same people as *quotquot . . . sumpserimus* in *Supplices*.[4] This is possible, and would give point to *quoque*, which it does not possess if it is regarded as following *Supplices* immediately, without the interposition of the *Memento* of the Dead. This reference to the clergy as *peccatores* can be paralleled in Eastern sources and in medieval commentators on the Roman Mass.

12. PER QUEM

Before the doxology of the great Eucharistic Prayer, beginning *Per*

[1] See B. Botte, *Le canon de la messe romaine*, Louvain, 1935, pp. 67–9; M. Andrieu, *Les Ordines Romani du haut moyen-âge*, II, 274–81, Louvain, 1948; "L'insertion du Memento des morts au canon romain de la messe", in *Revue des sciences religieuses*, I, pp. 151–7, Paris, 1921.

[2] See F. Cabrol, in *Paléographie musicale*, V, Solesmes, 1896, pp. 80–1.

[3] B. Botte, *Le Canon de la messe romaine*, Louvain, 1935, p. 69.

[4] J. A. Jungmann, *The Mass of the Roman Rite*, London, 1961, pp. 446–9.

ipsum et cum ipso et in ipso,[1] we find the relative clause

> Per quem haec omnia domine semper bona creas sanctificas uiuificas benedicis et praestas nobis.

As it stands in the Canon, it does not fit well with what precedes; for instance *haec omnia* is awkward if it refers only to the two eucharistic species of bread and wine. But it is known that it was at this place, the end of the Canon, before the doxology, that natural products were blessed on special occasions, for example the water, milk, and honey at solemn baptism,[2] the grapes on the feast of St Sixtus,[3] the oil on Maundy Thursday,[4] and the beans on Ascension Day.[5] In all these cases the proper prayer ends with a mention of Christ, and

> per quem haec omnia domine semper bona creas sanctificas uiuificas benedicis et praestas nobis

follows very smoothly.[6] Thus, in the Old Gelasian, on Maundy Thursday we have

> BENEDICTIO OLEI. *Ad populum in his uerbis:* Istud oleum ad unguendos infirmos. *Ut autem ueneris* Nobis quoque peccatoribus famulis tuis *et reliqua usque ad* Per Christum dominum nostrum. *Et intras:* Emitte, quaesumus, domine spiritum sanctum paraclytum de caelis in hac pinguedine olei . . . in nomine domini nostri Iesu Christi: per quem haec omnia, domine, semper bona creas. *Et cetera.*[7]

In summing up it may be said that Offertory, Thanksgiving, Intercession, Consecration, Anamnesis, and Oblation are all bound together in one great eucharistic prayer, have a natural sequence and a logical development, and make a satisfying unit. It is the two *Mementos* and *Nobis quoque* which are the items most difficult to fit into a coherent scheme.

[1] See F. Cabrol, in *Paléographie musicale*, V, Solesmes, 1896, pp. 81–3; C. Callewaert, "La finale du canon de la messe", in *R.H.E.*, 39 (1943), pp. 5–21.
[2] *Sacramentarium Veronense*, ed. L. C. Mohlberg, No. 205.
[3] *Gel.* III, lxxxviii, ed. Mohlberg, No. 1603.
[4] *Gel.*, I, xl, ed. Mohlberg, Nos, 381–2.
[5] *Gel.*, I, lxiii, ed. Mohlberg, No. 577; III, lxxxviii, ibid., No. 1603.
[6] J. A. Jungmann, *The Mass of the Roman Rite*, London, 1961, pp. 454–7.
[7] *Gel.*, I, xl, ed. Mohlberg, Nos. 381–2.

Bibliography

PRIMARY SOURCES

Pseudo-Alcuin, *De diuinis officiis*. P.L. 101, 1173–1286.
Amalarius, *De ecclesiasticis officiis*, ed. I. M. Hanssens, *Amalarii Episcopi Opera Liturgica Omnia*, t. II, Vatican City, 1948.
— *Epistula ad Hilduinum abbatem*, ed. I. M. Hannsens, op. cit. t. I, Vatican City, 1948.
Ambrose, *De Sacramentis*, ed. O. Faller, C.S.E.L., 73, Vienna, 1955.
Augustine, *De haeresibus*, P.L. 42.
— *Epistulae*, C.S.E.L., 34, 44, 57.
— *Sermones*, P.L. 38, 39, C.C. 41.
Bede, *Historia Ecclesiastica Gentis Anglorum*, ed. C. Plummer, Oxford, 1896.
Bernon of Reichenau, *Dialogus qualiter Quatuor Temporum ieiunia per sua sabbata sint obseruanda*, P.L. 142, 1087–98.
— *Libellus de quibusdam rebus ad missae officium pertinentibus*, P.L. 142, 1055–80.
Caesarius of Arles, *Sermones*, C.C. 103, 104.
Cyprian, *Epistulae*, C.S.E.L., 3.
De obseruatione quattuor temporum, ed. G. Morin, in *R.B.* 30, pp. 231–4.
Didascaliae apostolorum fragmenta ueronensia latina, ed. E. Hauler, Leipzig, 1900.
Egbert of York, *De institutione catholica dialogus*, P.L. 89, 435–42.
Epistulae Romanorum Pontificum, ed. Thiel, Braunsberg, 1868.
Eusebius, *Historia Ecclesiastica*, ed. G. Bardy, Paris, 1953; P.G. 67.
Gregory the Great, *Registrum Epistularum*, ed. Ewald-Hartmann, M.G.H. Epistulae, 1–2.
Innocent I, *Epistulae*, P.L. 20, 463–612.
Hippolytus, *Apostolic Tradition*, ed. B. Botte, Paris, 1946; ed. G. Dix, London, 1937.
Isidore of Seville, *De ecclesiasticis officiis*, P.L. 83, 739–826.
John the Deacon, *Vita Gregorii Magni*, P.L. 75, 63–242.
Justin Martyr, *Apology*, ed. I. C. T. Otto, Iena, 1876.
Leo the Great, *Epistulae*, P.L. 54, 593–1218.
— *Sermones*, P.L. 54, 141–463.
Liber Pontificalis, ed. L. Duchesne, I, Paris, 1884–6.

Liber precationum quas Carolus Calvus Imp . . . colligi . . . mandavit, ed. F. Felician, Ingolstadt, 1583.

Bernold of Constance, *Micrologus*, P.L. 151, 979–1022.

Origen, *In Matthaeum*, ed. E. Klostermann, *Origines Werke*, elfter Band, *Origenes Mattäuserklärung*, II, *Die lateinische Übersetzung der Commentariorum Series*, Leipzig, 1933.

Philaster, *De haeresibus*, P.L. 12, 1049–1288.

Prosper, *Contra Collatorem*, P.L. 51, 215–76.

—— *De uocatione omnium gentium*, P.L. 51, 647–722.

—— *Responsiones ad capitula obiectionum Vincentianarum*, P.L. 51, 177–86.

Serapion, *Sacramentary*, ed. G. Wobbermin, in *Texte und Untersuchungen*, XVII, Heft 3*b*, Leipzig, 1898.

Tertullian, *De Oratione*, C.S.E.L., 20; C.C. 1.

Victor of Vita, *Historia persecutionis Africanae prouinciae*, C.S.E.L., 7.

Walafrid Strabo, *Libellus de exordiis et incrementis in obseruationibus ecclesiasticis rerum*, P.L. 114, 919–66.

LITURGICAL TEXTS

EASTERN LITURGIES

F. E. Brightman, *Liturgies Eastern and Western*, I, *Eastern Liturgies*, Oxford, 1896.

WESTERN LITURGIES

ROMAN SACRAMENTARIES

(Leonine) L. C. Mohlberg, *Sacramentarium Veronense*, in Rerum Ecclesiasticarum Documenta, Fontes I, Rome, 1956.

(Gelasian) L. C. Mohlberg, *Liber Sacramentorum Romanae Aecclesiae Ordinis Anni circuli*, ibid., IV, Rome, 1960.

(Gregorian) (*Hadrianum*) H. Lietzmann, *Das Sacramentarium, Gregorianum nach dem Aachener Urexemplar*, Münster-in-Westfalen, 1921.

(*Paduense*) L. C. Mohlberg, *Die älteste erreichbare Gestalt des Liber Sacramentorum anni circuli der römischen Kirche*, Münster-in-Westfalen, 1927.

(*Alcuinianum*) H. A. Wilson, *The Gregorian Sacramentary under Charles the Great*, H.B.S., 49, London, 1915.

THE ROMAN CANON

B. Botte, *Le canon de la messe romaine*, Louvain, 1935.

L. Eizenhöfer, *Canon missae romanae*, Rome, 1954.

THE ROMAN ORDINES

M. Andrieu, *Les ordines romani du haut Moyen-Age*, 5 vols., Louvain, 1931–61.

THE ANTIPHONARY

R. J. Hesbert, *Antiphonale Missarum Sextuplex*, Brussels, 1935.

NON-ROMAN RITES

Bobbio Missal, ed. E. A. Lowe, H.B.S., 58, 61, London, 1920, 1923.

Liber Ordinum, ed. M. Férotin, in *Monumenta Ecclesiae Liturgica*, V, Paris, 1904.

Missale Gothicum, ed. L. C. Mohlberg, in Rerum Ecclesiasticarum Documenta, Fontes V, Rome 1961; ed. H. M. Banister, in H.B.S., 52, 54, London, 1917, 1919.

Missale mixtum, P.L. 85.

Stowe Missal, ed. G. F. Warner, H.B.S., 32, London. 1915.

SECONDARY SOURCES

Alfonzo, P., *Oratio Fidelium*, Finalpia, 1928.

Andrieu, M., "A propos de quelques sacramentaires récemment édités", in *Revue des sciences religieuses*, 2, Paris, 1922, pp. 190–210.

— "L'insertion du Memento des morts au canon romain de la messe", in *Revue des sciences religieuses*, I, pp. 151–4, Paris, 1921.

Baumstark, A., *Comparative Liturgy*, revised by B. Botte, E.T. by F. L. Cross, London, 1958.

— "Liturgischer Nachall der Verfolgungszeit" in A. M. Koeniger, *Beiträge zur Geschichte des christlichen Altertums und der byzantinischen Literatur, Festgabe Albert Ehrhard*, Bonn-Leipzig, 1922, pp. 53–72.

— *Missale Romanum*, Eindhoven, 1929.

Botte, B. and Mohrmann, C., *L'ordinaire de la messe*, Paris-Louvain, 1953.

Biehl, L., *Das liturgische Gebet für Kaiser und Reich*, Paderborn, 1937.

Bishop, E., *Liturgica Historica*, Oxford, 1918.

Bishop, E., and Wilmart, A., *Le génie du rite romain*, Paris, 1920.

Bourque, E., *Etudes sur les sacramentaires romains*, Rome, 1948.

Brightman, F. E., *The English Rite*, London, 1915.

Brou, L., "Etude historique sur les oraisons des dimanches après la Pentecôte dans la tradition romaine", in *Sacris Erudiri*, II, 1949, pp. 123–223.

— "Une ancienne station romaine à Saint-Pierre pour le dimanche précédant les Quatre-Temps", in *E.L.*, 60, Rome 1946, pp. 143–50.

Cabrol, F., "Annonce des fêtes", in *D.A.C.L.*, I, 2230–41.

— "Canon romain" in *D.A.C.L.*, II, 1847–1905.

Callewaert, C., "Les étapes de l'histoire du Kyrie: s. Gélase, s. Benoît, s. Grégoire", in *R.H.E.*, 38, pp. 20–45, Louvain, 1942.

— "La finale du canon de la messe", in *R.H.E.*, 39, pp. 5–21.

— "La semaine *mediana* dans l'ancien carême romain et les Quatre-Temps", in *R.B.*, 36 (1924), pp. 22 ff., reprinted in *Sacris Erudiri*, 1940, pp. 584–8.

— "S. Léon, le *Communicantes* et le *Nobis quoque peccatoribus*", in *Sacris Erudiri*, I, Bruges, 1948, pp. 123–64.

— "S. Léon le Grand et les textes du Léonien", in *Sacris Erudiri*, I, Bruges, 1948, pp. 71–8.

Capelle, B., "Antiennes pour la moisson dans le missel romain", in *Q.L.P.*, XIV, Louvain, 1929, pp. 163–7.

— *Travaux liturgiques de doctrine et d'histoire*, II, *Histoire. La messe*, Louvain, 1962.

Cappuyns, M., "L'auteur du 'De Vocatione Omnium Gentium' ", in *R.B.*, 39, Maredsous, 1927, pp. 198–226.

— "L'origine des *Capitula* pseudo-célestiens contre le semi-pélagianisme", in *R.B.*, 41, Maredsous, 1929, pp. 156–70.

— "Les *Orationes Sollemnes* du vendredi saint", in *Q.L.P.*, 23, Louvain, 1938, pp. 18–31.

Chavasse, A., "L'avent romain du VIe au VIIIe siècle", in *E.L.*, 67, Rome, 1953, pp. 297–308.

— "La préparation à la Pâque, à Rome, avant le Ve siècle: Jeûne et organisation liturgique", in *Mémorial J. Chaine*, Lyon, 1950, pp. 61–80.

— *Le sacramentaire gélasien*, Tournai, 1958.

— "Les messes quadragésimales du sacramentaire gélasien Vat. Reg. 316", in *E.L.*, 63, Rome, 1949, pp. 257–75.

— "Les plus anciens types du lectionnaire et de l'antiphonaire romains de la messe", in *R.B.*, 62, Maredsous, 1952, pp. 3–94.

— "Messes du pape Gélase dans le sacramentaire léonien", in *R.B.*, 56, Maredsous, 1945–6, pp. 12–41.

— "Retouches gélasiennes dans le sacramentaire léonien", in *R.B.*, 61, Maredsous, 1951, pp. 3–14.

Chavoutier, L., "Un libellus pseudo-ambrosien sur le Saint-Esprit", in *Sacris Erudiri*, 11, Bruges, 1960, pp. 136–92.

Clark, A. C., *The cursus in Medieval and Vulgar Latin*, Oxford, 1910.

— *Fontes Prosae Numerosae*, Oxford, 1909.

Connolly, R. H., "Liturgical Prayers of Intercession, I: The Good Friday 'Orationes Sollemnes' ", in *J.T.S.* 21, Oxford, 1920, pp. 219 ff.

Cross, F. L., "Pre-Leonine Elements in the Proper of the Roman Mass", in *J.T.S.*, 50, Oxford, 1949, pp. 191–7.

Delehaye, H., "Martyr et confesseur", in *Analecta Bollandiana*, 39, pp. 20–49, Brussels, 1921.

Dix, G., *The Shape of the Liturgy*, Westminster, 1945.

Duchesne, L., *Christian Worship*, E.T., 5th ed., London, 1931.

Dugmore, C. W., *The influence of the Synagogue upon the Divine Office*, Oxford, 1944.

Elbogen, J., *Studien zur Geschichte des jüdischen Gottesdienstes*, (*Schriften der Lehranstalt für die Wissenschaft des Judenthums*, Band I, Heft 1, 2) Berlin, 1907.

Ellard, G., "Interpolated Amens in the Canon of the Mass", in *Theological Studies*, VI, U.S.A., 1945, pp. 380–91.

Feltoe, C. L., "Adversaria Liturgica, A. 'Mediana Hebdomada Quadragesimae' " in *J.T.S.*, 2, Oxford, 1901, pp. 130–7.

Fortescue, A., *The Mass: A Study of the Roman Liturgy*, London, 1937.

Frere, W. H., *Studies in Early Roman Liturgy*, Alcuin Club Collections 27, 28, and 30, Oxford, 1930–5.

Janini, J., *S. Siricio y las cuatro temporas*, Valencia, 1958.

Jungmann, J. A., "Die Quadragesima in den Forschungen von A. Chavasse", in *Archiv für Liturgiewissenschaft* 5 (1957), pp. 84–95.

— *The early Liturgy to the time of Gregory the Great*, London, 1960.

— *Missarum Sollemnia*, 2nd ed., Freiburg, 1958.

(American translation) *The Mass of the Roman Rite*, London, 1961.

Kennedy V. L., "The pre-Gregorian 'Hanc igitur' ", in *E.L.*, 1936, pp. 349–58.

— "The two collects of the Gelasian", in *Miscellanea Liturgica in honorem L. Cuniberti Mohlberg*, I, pp. 183–8, Rome, 1948.

de Labriolle, P., "Une exquisse de l'histoire du mot 'Papa' ", in *Bulletin d'ancienne littérature et d'archéologie chrétiennes*, I, Paris, 1911, pp. 215–20.

Lambot, C., "Le Pater dans la liturgie apostolique d'après s. Grégoire", in *R.B.*, 42, Maredsous, 1930, pp. 265–9.

Laurand, L., *Ce qu'on sait et ce qu'on ignore du Cursus,* Louvain-Paris, 1914.

Leclercq, H., "Cursus", in *D.A.C.L.*, III, cols. 3193 ff.

Lowe, E. A., *Codices Latini Antiquiores* VI, Oxford, 1953.

Maertens, T., "L'avent", in *Mélanges de science religieuse*, 18, Lille, 1961, pp. 47–110.

Martimort, A. G., (ed.) *L'église en prière*, Paris, 1961.

Mohrmann, C., "Quelques observations sur l'évolution stylistique du canon de la messe romaine", in *Vigiliae Christianae*, 4, Amsterdam, 1950, pp. 1–19.

Morin, G., "L'origine des Quatre-Temps", in *R.B.*, 14, pp. 337–46.

— "Notes d'ancienne littérature chrétienne. I. Que faut-il entendre par les confessores auxquels était addressé le traité de Macrobe le donatiste?" in *R.B.*, 29, Maredsous, 1912, pp. 82–4.

Nicolau, M. G., *L'origine du Cursus rythmique et les débuts de l'accent d'intensité en latin*, Paris, 1930.

Ratcliff, E. C., "Christian Worship and Liturgy", in K. E. Kirk, *The Study of Theology*, London, 1932, pp. 409–80.

— "The Institution Narrative of the Roman *Canon Missae*; Its beginnings and early background", in *Studia Patristica,* II, pp. 64–82, *Texte und Untersuchungen*, 64, Berlin, 1957.

Salmon, P., "Les 'Amen' du canon de la messe", in *E.L.*, 42, Rome, 1928, pp. 496–506.

Schmidt, H. A. P., *Hebdomada Sancta*, Rome, 1957.

Schuster, I., *The Sacramentary* (*Liber Sacramentorum*), E.T., London, 1924 ff.

Srawley, J. H., *The Early History of the Liturgy*, 2nd ed., Cambridge 1947.

Steuart, B., *The Development of Christian Worship*, London, 1953.

Tellenbach, G., *Römischer und christlicher Reichsgedanke in der Liturgie des frühen M.A.*, in *Sitzungsberichte* (Acad. de Heidelberg, Phil.-Hist. Kl.). 1934, pp. 4–54.

Turner, C. H., "The Papal Chronology of the third century, 3. Antiquity of the rule of Sunday ordination", in *J.T.S.*, 17, Oxford, 1916, pp. 341 ff.

Vacandard, E., "Le cursus: son origine, son histoire, son emploi dans la liturgie", in *Revue des questions historiques*, 78, Paris, 1905, pp. 59–102.

Wilmart, A., *Le Lectionnaire d'Alcuin*, Rome, 1937.

Indexes

Proper Names

The Ordinary of the Roman Mass

Ordines Romani

THE ALCUIN CLUB—of which Dr Walter Howard Frere was for many years the President—exists for the object of promoting the study of the History and Use of the Book of Common Prayer and Christian Liturgies. It encourages, by publications and other means, the practical study of the English liturgy with its ceremonial, and the arrangement of churches, their furniture, and ornaments, in accordance with the rubrics of the Book of Common Prayer, strict obedience to which is the guiding principle of the work of the Club. During the last half-century the Alcuin Club has issued some hundred publications—Collections, Smaller Books, Pamphlets, and Leaflets—and Members of the Club are entitled to the publications of the current year *gratis*. The subscription for Members is 21*s*. per annum. Application for election and for the List of Publications should be sent to the Assistant Secretary, as well as all subscriptions.

President

THE RIGHT REVEREND J. W. C. WAND, K.C.V.O., D.D.

Chairman

THE REV. CANON W. K. LOWTHER CLARKE, D.D.

Committee

THE RIGHT REV. D. C. DUNLOP, M.A.
PROFESSOR I. L. FOSTER, M.A., F.S.A.
THE REV. R. C. D. JASPER, D.D., F.R.HIST.S.
THE REV. M. R. J. MANKTELOW, M.A.
THE REV. C. E. POCKNEE, A.K.C.
THE REV. H. B. PORTER, PH.D.
DR F. J. E. RABY, C.B., LITT.D., F.B.A.
THE REV. G. G. WILLIS, PH.D.
THE REV. G. B. TIMMS, M.A., *Hon. Treasurer*
THE REV. F. C. WALDEN-ASPY, M.A., *Hon. Secretary*
St James' Vicarage, Littlehampton, Sussex

Assistant Secretary and Treasurer

MISS W. K. MEDWAY, c/o Theological Department, King's College, Strand, London W.C.2